holidays FROM HELL

IMPORTANT NOTE

Although all these stories were transmitted on the TV show *Holidays from Hell,* many of the holidays described were taken several years ago and the operations of the companies concerned may have changed.

holidays FROM HELL

Dominic Wills

GRANADA

First published in Great Britain in 2003
By Granada Media, an imprint of André Deutsch Limited
20 Mortimer Street
London W1T 3JW

Holidays From Hell is a Granada Production

A catalogue record is available from the British Library

ISBN 0 233 00042 9

Typeset by E-Type, Liverpool

Printed and bound in Great Britain

2 4 6 8 10 9 7 5 3 1

contents

Introduction

For most people, holidays are the stuff of memories. Indeed, for those of us of a certain age, the memory is all we have – the Polaroids having disintegrated while being held too long and tightly in a sweaty armpit. For us, holidays flood back as balmy reminders of an age of innocence, when we were but children and way too self-centred to notice the dreadful problems of the adults surrounding us. Looking back, those hazy summer days seem to melt into one another. There we are, sitting on a damp towel on the smooth pebbles, sucking strawberry-flavoured ice from a plastic tube that cuts the corners of your mouth, watching Dad bob up and down on the glittering water, his arms and legs dangling over the sides of an inflatable dinghy made for a six-year-old.

These are the days we appreciate most, the ones we plan and dream about. We pore for days over catalogues, seeking our place in the sun. We quiz our friends, surf the

Net, we even subject ourselves to hours of telly where smug sub-celebrities loll about in exotic locales, enjoying vacations we couldn't possibly afford, usually paid for with money we dished out for our TV licence.

Holidays can mean so many different things to different people. For the young and curious, they can be an early mind-opening experience. With a ruck-sack carelessly stuffed with cool shades, swimming gear, shorts, teeshirt, perhaps a sarong and maybe two pairs of smalls (in case of accident), they can set out to see the world, drink in new cultures and make full use of other countries' varying attitudes to intoxicants. The young and decadent can go in search of sun, sea and sex, goaded on to ever more revolting extremes by couriers apparently earning a commission from every spray of vomit and every condom used (either shredded in drunken coitus or split while being worn as a comedy mask).

For couples, holidays can be a chance to kindle or re-kindle that loving feeling, to set themselves against a back-drop of high romance, like Venice or Paris, to see themselves once more as Cathy and Heathcliff, tossed upon turbulent waves of passion in an appropriately gothic setting. For parents, holidays are an escape from the daily grind, where they can relax in the bosom of their immediate family. How sweet it is, light years away from the nerve-shredding stress of cooking, cleaning, juggling credit cards and ferrying the little monsters from ballet to football to mime to swimming to tennis and all the other classes they really ought to be taking during school-hours. Well, it's sweet until the little brats start begging for Cornettos and chips and crisps and cheap plastic footballs and counterfeit David Beckham shirts and more Cornettos, and then vomit all over your spanking new espadrilles.

These days, with flights being so much cheaper, we go so much further afield, to destinations our parents would have regarded with deep suspicion, if not xenophobic dislike, places whose customs and traditions we neither know nor understand. With the tourist industry being so much more lucrative, the competition to provide us with accommodation is like a shark-feeding frenzy. Inevitably, all manner of spivs and crooks are clamouring for your custom. Beyond this, machinery has advanced incredibly, such that we can now sail, ride and fly at absurdly high speeds on the most outlandish devices. We can go anywhere, do anything, and we do, often after having drunk far too much for our own good. Is it any wonder disasters occasionally befall us?

Which brings us to the subject of this book – those poor wretches for whom all did not go well, whose holiday memories do not arrive as summer-scented visions, but as black clouds of humiliation, horror and despair. These people have suffered disease and near-fatal injury. They've endured terrible privations. They've had their lives endangered by fires at sea, on land and in the air. They've cowered under the mighty force of hurricanes and struggled in the terrifying grip of the ocean. They've been harassed, threatened, lied to, manipulated and even beaten up. They've been sent to the wrong hotel. They've been sent to the right hotel, only to find it wasn't built yet. One couple even watched their hotel collapse at their feet. And there are so many more stories herein, all with one thing in common. These people's vacations have turned out to be vastly different from the pleasant dream they signed up to. Incidentally, all the names have been changed to protect the innocent.

Yet don't make the mistake of thinking this book is just about comedy gaffes, silly accidents and hilarious misfortunes. Much more of human experience is covered here. There's heroism and panic, deep tolerance and righteous anger, there's foolishness, greed, abject carelessness and outright wickedness. There is much to laugh about, more if your humour is particularly black. But some of these stories contain genuine tragedy. People are really hurt. People are really traumatised. People really die.

So while you read, think on this: as the man with the enormous finger said, It Could Be You.

1 Accidents will happen

They say that most accidents happen in the home, and that sounds reasonable enough. Most of us, for instance, get our electrics and carpeting done as cheaply as possible. It should come as no surprise that so many should tumble down the stairs, or ricochet off the ceiling. There are other dangers, too, many of them arising when engaging in a spot of DIY. How many thousand nails have been blackened by clumsy hammering? How many miles of skin have had to be tugged from the flesh due to the over-zealous use of Superglue? Peril even lurks in the food cupboard. We may be able to store the country's entire banking system on a tiny chip, but still we can't open a can of corned beef without half-severing our thumb.

Yes, home is where the ambulance is. Yet at home we can also get help. Things are infinitely more complicated (and scary) when you get hurt or sick abroad, as the following stories most graphically reveal.

CHAPTER ONE

The one with the little blue booties

James and Anita Simpson, an active couple in the prime of life, decided to take a trip skiing with friends in Colorado. Conditions were perfect. The sun shone brightly and a thick covering of the white powdery stuff gave everyone a chance to glide serenely down the picturesque mountainsides. Or maybe to storm down them at absurdly high speeds, shouting 'I am the Hermanator, and I'll be back!'

Unfortunately, these few perfect days on the slopes took their toll on James, and he began to feel a bit of discomfort in his back. He thought perhaps it was something to do with a heavy fall he'd taken the day before. He thought differently when he suddenly collapsed, clutching his chest, as waves of terrible pain rolled through him, stealing his breath and near paralysing him.

Anita rang the local medical centre immediately and James was taken straight in. It was a major drama. 'It was a bit surreal, really,' recalled James later with admirable humour. ' One minute you're sight-seeing in Denver, the next you're starring in ER'. Within minutes of arrival he was flat on his back in a hospital bed, wired up to an ECG machine, two drips, a blood-pressure cuff, an oxygen tank and God knows what else. All his clothes were removed but his trousers and pants. Despite all the heavy machinery, though, Anita remained fairly unconcerned. She really expected the doctors, as they traditionally do in the UK, to pack James back off to the hotel with a jar of paracetamol and casual instructions to come back in the morning if it wasn't all better.

But things were moving much faster than Anita imagined. Indeed, while she was sitting in the medical centre's waiting room, James had already been whisked off to a bigger hospital in Denver. For him life had become a rollercoaster. With absolutely no control over any aspect of anything at all, he found himself racing down the highway in a speeding ambulance, zipped onto a trolley and whizzed at running pace down endless corridors, doors crashing in front and behind, lights flashing by overhead. Finally he was laid to rest in another bed and wired up to a new array of bewilderingly complex machines. At last he had a chance to call Anita and let her know what was occurring – he was to be kept in overnight for tests. Everything was OK, the doctors were being very thorough. We've all heard about the efficiency of American doctors. They'll test the poop out of you – sometimes quite literally.

Unbeknownst to James, though, everything wasn't going to stay OK. Overnight, Colorado suffered its heaviest snowfall in a decade. The Interstate was shut down, as was the Eisenhower Tunnel. There was one road from Denver back to James's holiday resort and, though under normal circumstances it was a fine road, no one was quite sure where it was any more.

This was the situation when James awoke the next morning. He was feeling better, back to his old cheerful self, and was further delighted when nurse Megan informed him that all the tests had returned negative. It was probably just a muscle strain, no reason for concern. Hip hip hurray. Time to get back to those spectacular rolling slopes and perhaps a slap-up surf'n'turf lunch, by way of celebration.

But this, of course, was not to be. With the roads blocked by a hundred million tons of snow, neither Anita nor their friends could come to pick him up. In fact, having been informed about his clean bill of health, and believing him to be in good hands, they were happily toasting him before a raging log fire. Worse still, having been stripped of all his clothes back at the medical centre, he had no money, and no credit cards. He also lacked a coat, a shirt, and his shoes and socks. Poor old James – he's alone, broke and half-naked in the middle of a snowy state's worst snowstorm in ten years. As his American hosts might have had it, this *sucked.*

Happily, nurse Megan had a heart of gold and scuttled off to arrange some alternative clothing and accommodation in Denver. And alternative it certainly turned out to be. Within the hour, James, now clad in the baby-blue over-shoe booties that staff wear in operating theatres, a paper gown and a small blanket, and carrying his pathetic possessions in a plastic bag, found himself buzzing on the intercom of a hostel packed with hobos and, for all he knew, psychotic repeat offenders. Was he about to find out exactly what you do in Denver when you're dead? He felt, he later recalled, like Paddington Bear – but without the marmalade sandwiches. But angels come in all shapes and sizes and one of them worked at the hostel, ordering James a takeaway Chinese. So there he spent the night, sitting in his blue booties and paper gown, eating his dinner out of a cardboard box. How relieved was he, when the rescue party arrived the next day?

Yet there was more to come. On their return home, James and Anita began to receive a flood of bills from Colorado. $1300 for the radiologist, $2000 for the blood test, $200 for checking radioactivity in the lungs, on and on it went. Crazy figures. The holiday had cost £1300, and now the medical bills were coming in at $6000. Now, we all know that American medics check your wallet before your pulse, but James and Anita had asked at the medical centre and the hospital and had been told, quite categorically, that the insurance company had been contacted and would be covering all expenses.

But Primary Insurance wouldn't be covering all expenses. They didn't have to. For in the small print of James and Anita's policy it said the company was not liable if the insured failed to contact them within 24 hours of the illness. And this they had not done.

Fortunately, Primary did eventually cough up the dough, but James and Anita had learned a salutary lesson. Read your insurance policy carefully. This is your responsibility. Don't leave it with the tour operator, half of them can't even get it together to organise the flight. It's *your* responsibility. Otherwise it could be you out there under the Big Sky, with nothing but a paper gown between you and the screaming, freezing elements, weeing on yourself for warmth. A bad show – avoid it.

The one with the cascading iodine

Alison MacDonald and her partner John Bentley fancied a holiday with a difference, something a little classier than usual, something to simultaneously feed the brain and set the senses racing. And where better than Egypt, home of the Pharaohs, the mighty Sphinx and the pyramids, those pointy wonders of the ancient world? Keen to soak in the dramatic history of the place, they spent the first week on a boat down the Nile, occasionally stopping off to view the temples, marvel at the extensive excavations and wonder at the strange and bloody histories behind the endless hieroglyphics. Their second week they planned to spend on a slow, relaxing exploration of the city of Luxor.

Luxor – what a region to explore. Just down the road is

Thebes, the fabled Hecatompylos, ancient capital of the country. In its days of splendour it extended twenty-three miles and possessed a hundred gates, through each of which, in times of distress, could pour two hundred chariots and twenty thousand fighting men. Naturally, it was not often anyone thought to cause Thebes distress – they kicked ancient ass. To the east, across the white desert, lies the Red Sea. To the west, cross another desert to the Great Oasis and you find yourself in the midst of the Great Sand Sea and the fearsome Sahara itself. Travel south and you soon reach the monumental Aswan Dam and the vast expanse of Lake Nasser, taking you down into Sudan.

An amazing place, and Luxor itself is a wonder, too. Alison and John arrived at their beautifully appointed hotel looking forward to a week full of exotic discoveries and modern high-living. Entering their hotel room they looked out across a picture postcard view, stretching out across pretty white marinas busy with white-sailed yachts, over the blue, blue Nile to palm trees swaying in the wind, and the sweeping sand dunes of the west bank. The sun was out, they recall, it was gorgeous, you couldn't hope for better weather.

In fact, it was too gorgeous, and a healthy spot of English drizzle might well have prevented what came next. Crossing the room towards the shimmering brightness of the balcony, Alison suddenly heard a loud cracking noise around her. As she pulled back, shocked and fearful, a large piece of glass slid down in front of her like a guillotine. She felt it slip past her nose and chin and straight down the front of her body, before it smacked against the bottom of the door and shattered into vicious smithereens. Looking down, she was horrified to see that her formerly tanned and pristine legs and feet were now coated entirely in her own blood.

Immediately, an ambulance was called. John explained to the tour reps that both he and Alison had private medical insurance and off they sped to one of the city's finer private hospitals. Or so they thought. In fact, seconds after the ambulance shrieked to a halt, Alison and John found themselves rushed into the bowels of the infamous Luxor General. And now the screaming started. They thought it looked ominous when the operating theatre turned out to be a small room, empty apart from a table with a cloth over it. The doctor, though, looked professional enough. Little did they know he'd actually graduated from the Josef Mengele School of Medicine. After a cursory examination of Alison's deepest wound, a cut on her shin that John claimed had exposed an area of bone the size of his fist, the doctor hummed a bit, ha-ed a tad, and then poured a bottle of neat iodine directly onto the gaping sore!

Just the thought of this induces a sharp intake of breath and has you scrunching your face into one big wrinkle. So imagine poor Alison. She howled and nearly hit the ceiling. It was, she said later 'as if my leg was being set alight and at the same time somebody was trying to saw it off'. Ouch. And then Double-Ouch as the scene reached a pinnacle of pain worthy of the Marquis de Sade. The doctor, recognising that the neat iodine had left the job only half-done, now proceeded to stitch up her shin. Or rather, he *attempted* to stitch up her shin – he had a bit of trouble getting the needle through her skin. Several times. Poor, poor Alison – she lay there watching it all. At this point, she said, she was begging to be knocked out, 'I was regretting surviving the accident'. And poor John. He, too, was entirely helpless, utterly unable to soothe his tortured beloved. All he could do was pin her to the table and minimise her agonised writhing, so the doctor wouldn't make many more holes than were strictly necessary. It is without doubt that local medics thousands of years before would have made a better job of it.

Eventually, those nice people at Luxor General dropped the couple in a cab back to the hotel. And at last Luck smiled on them, in the shape of a notice saying the next flight to Manchester had been delayed by two hours. If they could reach the airport in ten minutes, they could be on it. Piling into a cab, they waved £50 worth of Egyptian notes at the driver and gave him his deadline. He took off like a bat out of Hell, and then got quicker, making their destination in fine time. Then – disaster! – with the minutes running desperately short, the Thomson rep who had to sign the form allowing them to board needed to know all the details of the accident. Sharply officious, the rep demanded to know it all, at one point laying pen to pad and fixing them with an unforgiving stare.

How they made it onto the plane is anyone's guess, but make it they did. And a few hours later Alison was being whisked by a British fire-crew into the gentle arms of the British medical service. 'Britain,' she remembers thinking at that point, 'is the best place in the world to be'. A touch of the Candides there, you suspect, but you get where she's coming from.

As it turned out, Alison was one of very few who ever receive reasonable compensation for the troubles they suffer on vacation. As they were leaving their Luxor hotel, she and John noticed the staff putting stickers up on the windows and glass doors – stickers they'd obviously possessed all along but not bothered to employ. Also, the glass that had made such a grotesque mess of Alison's shin was found to be only four millimetres thick, two less than Egypt's standard requirement. The couple had paid £800 for their furlough in Hades. Alison settled out of court with Thomson for £100,000. She's lucky to be alive to spend it. If she had not stepped back when she heard that glass crack, she'd have been buried in two thin coffins.

The ones with all the poo

As far as holidays go, all-inclusive packages can go well. But when they go badly, they bring with them more than a whiff of the Infernal Regions. Indeed, industry insiders reckon that about 90% of all complaints are about such packages. The Pickford family were not aware of this when they booked their trip to Mallorca with Sun World, neither were the Hall family. Both took up all-inclusive holidays to Club Aguamar, hoping to reap the benefits of free food, free drinks and the club's 'unique cabaret', an ongoing show often involving nude men covering their privates with small white plates. Relaxation was supposed to be the name of the game.

The first day went well. The sun was hot, the food was good and, more importantly, the kids agreed to eat it. But Day 2 was a different proposition altogether. A mean and malodorous day it was. Both families found themselves struck down with the most virulent of stomach complaints. There was diarrhoea, vomiting, shivers, stomach ache, back ache, a catalogue of cruel complaints. Mrs Hall claimed the pain was worse than labour, though the issue was rather less solid. Mrs Pickford described how her husband was so drained he was almost paralysed, while her youngest child, confused and frightened by this new and violent need to poop, screamed in the bathroom and passed out. She had to get the doctor. Racing downstairs, she noticed there was no one round the pool, where the previous day there'd been hundreds. The missing hundreds she discovered in reception, most of them holding very poorly children and all of them complaining vociferously. One woman reported that her husband was in bed howling with fear at the things he saw crawling from the walls.

Sun World reps called a meeting of all the guests, which was heavily attended and quickly turned ugly. The guests expected Sun World to explain what was happening and what they were doing about it. When a doctor came onstage and told them that the hotel's food was fine, they'd just all caught a virus, they were livid. Well, even more livid. One man strode up to the doctor, snatched his microphone and threw it off into the corner, the doctor was quickly led to safety by staff. Three days later, it was announced that the outbreak had been caused by salmonella, but the hotel was now clear of it.

Back in Blighty, Sharon Southgate heard about the outbreak from a friend who'd just got back from Mallorca. As she too was booked in at Club Aguamar, she called her travel agent to check that all was now well. She didn't want to take a chance, especially not with her young baby. The agent was most convincing. There was no cause for concern. Indeed, what with the rigorous checks, it was now probably the safest place on the island. Six days later, ensconced at the safest place on the island, baby Vicky exploded from both ends. To Sharon's horror, the doctor wouldn't say what was wrong, he just told them to order an ambulance immediately. The baby was in chronic pain, suffering from a virus usually associated with improper food hygiene. At the hospital, Sharon, fearing for her child's life, discovered that three babies had been admitted that week, all suffering the same symptoms.

Due to the outbreak, Holiday Travelwatch was inundated with almost 1000 calls, and believed the Club Aguamar problem to be the worst case of food poisoning ever to strike British travellers abroad. There would be some serious and organised demands for compensation, with people threatening the biggest legal action ever against a British tour operator. Most of the complainants had suffered in the same outbreak, but they were joined by Paul and Linda Perkin, guests at Club Aguamar the year before. Linda, in fact, was still on medication due to the condition she picked up at the hotel (some can stay with you for life). Their description of their all-in family holiday beggars belief. At one point, someone was vomiting in the sink, someone else in the bath, another in the toilet, and a fourth in the bidet. Paul described trying to cross the room to give his children medication, or water to prevent them dehydrating, with diarrhoea running down his legs. They felt utterly inadequate as parents, asking themselves why had they brought their children into this revolting hell-hole, and what could they possibly do to help them?

Paul called Sun World reps, demanding an explanation. They stated quite categorically that the Perkins had brought the bug with them. Yet around 50% of the guests were suffering the same agonies. It's amazing their plane didn't fall out of the sky, what with the weight of all those viruses stowing away on board. On their return to the UK, the Perkins demanded financial redress and were offered £250. Asking Thomas Cook whether this was adequate, they were told it was a good offer. When they turned it down and were instead offered £350, the Thomas Cook people said it was a *great* offer. Imagine the look on Paul's face when he discovered that Sun World were owned by – yes, you've guessed it – Thomas Cook.

The one with the dangerous window

As mentioned above, they say most accidents occur at home and the theory certainly holds water. Home is, after all, where we live. But plenty of accidents also take place while people are on holiday, and that makes a lot of sense, too. Even disregarding people who like to spend their vacations trying to break the record for the fastest descent of Everest while sliding on your naked bottom, holidays can be downright dangerous. We don't know the terrain, we don't know what's round the next corner, and we've probably had way too much to drink. It is, you will agree, a recipe for disaster.

And even people who don't drink can find themselves in dreadful straits. Take Kirsty Holmes, who took a holiday on Tenerife with her partner Roland and daughters Michelle and Jade. The plan was to spend Christmas and New Year at the Hotel Oro Negro, and the plan was good. The staff would entertain the kids, putting on carol concerts and pantomimes, and running sports competitions with darts, snooker, the lot. The kids loved it, especially Jade, and Christmas had been fantastic.

Then it happened. As New Year approached, Steve Parlour and his mate Pete Irwin, both lads in their twenties, were enjoying a game of snooker. There were little kids running all over the place, but the lads were too engrossed in their duel upon the green baize to worry. Then Steve, about to play a shot, saw out of the corner of his eye a little girl run behind him. He expected her to then appear in the corner of his other eye, but she never did. He completed his shot and, curious over the incident, asked Pete if he'd seen the little girl pass. He had not. Steve turned around, bemused. All there was behind him was an open window with the curtains blowing outwards. Weird.

And then the horrible realisation struck them both at once. They went to the window and looked down. There, some forty feet below, lay the phantom girl. Steve told

Pete to call an ambulance and then took off downstairs. He started at manic speed but, he said later, began to slow down as the thought hit him of what he might be running towards. And there she was, little Jade, curled up in a ball on the ground with blood coming out of her ears.

Following his friend down, having called for help, Pete met a woman coming up the stairs who said she thought Jade was dead. In reception, he saw another woman. It was Kirsty. He asked her if she had a little girl. She said yes and, before she'd even heard the terrible news, she went instantly into hysterics. She had read the absolute worst on his face.

Then came a shout from outside. It was Steve, demanding someone call an ambulance as Jade was still alive. You can only imagine Kirsty's feelings at this point. And also when she arrived at the hospital to discover that none of the medics spoke English and could not let her know how her daughter was. When a Thomson rep arrived she pounced on him, desperate for information. But he couldn't speak Spanish. No one, she believed, had been trained for this kind of crisis. Her torment would continue throughout the seven days Jade spent in intensive care.

Jade's accident could easily have been avoided. The window through which she fell was some eight feet high, but with only about two feet of brick coming off the floor. It was a simple business to trip and fall, particularly for a child infused with the holiday spirit. The hotel would quickly screw the window shut and place a net below, to prevent any catastrophic repeat.

Jade, thankfully, made a compete recovery and Kirsty recognised how lucky she was. Lucky to have survived such a fall, and lucky that Steve, lacking the intensity of Peter Ebdon, had not been so focused on his game that he missed the sudden and mystifying disappearance of a small child. Yvonne wasn't lucky enough to win compensation, though. She'd paid £2456 for her fear-ridden vacation. Thomson just said they were sorry.

2 All creatures great and microscopic

We're an arrogant lot, we humans. We think we can clear off any plot of land to build our houses and hotels, and the original inhabitants will just go away and leave us to it. How very wrong we are. Take badgers, for example. They have paths they like to follow – runs, they're called – and they stick to them stubbornly. One bloke inadvertently built a house on a badger's run and, when it was completed, woke one night to find the badger had forced its way through the cat-flap and, discovering the other end of his run to be blocked, was busily ripping up the kitchen. Animals don't always run away from us. Often our presence – as with foxes and rats – only helps them multiply. Plants are the same. We may think we clear them away but they're still there, their seeds and spores hiding in our walls and our gardens, waiting for their chance to burst forth once again. They look upon our works and they do not despair.

The following Holidays from Hell show many of the different ways other creatures can ruin our fun. There are big scary animals, small creepy insects, and even tiny fungi, individually almost invisible to the human eye, but fearsome when they get together in a huge gang. All of them have their own special ways to poop the party.

The one with the hungry, hungry hippos

Stella Thomson and Rod Dawson liked a good adventure. They'd been to some wild places before, but now they felt ready for the big one – Africa, the renowned root of civilisation. They didn't want to go on their own. 'Having been abroad before,' explained Stella, 'I know how deep into trouble you can get if you're simply naïve'. This was why they chose tour operator African Routes, a firm that offered the opportunity to witness exotic creatures in their natural habitat in Swaziland, a real grass roots experience.

And it all began well. Their guide for the tour was Gunter, an affable sort who jollied up the party, telling them they'd be up early, that they'd make fools of themselves, but that they would certainly party hearty, Marty. Yet as the days passed cheery Gunter became moody, miserable even. He slept a lot and kept driving past places of interest. Indeed, his erratic and sometimes unpleasant behaviour became a joke on the tour. Then, one day Stella noticed that he was trembling in the front of the truck. Slipping down to investigate, she noticed that he was wrapped in four layers of clothing, all of them soaked. The party had thought he was enjoying a crafty fag. In fact, he was *steaming*.

Taking a detour to a nearby hospital, they unloaded the wretched guide, by now as catatonic as a zombie, into a wheelchair and rolled him inside. Unfortunately, though he had a severe case of malaria, he *didn't* have insurance and so the doctors pumped him full of drugs and put him back in the truck. Just the kind of guy you want guiding you when the lions are about to pounce, eh?

But there was help at hand. In keeping with the glorious tradition of Steven Seagal, Mary the cook took over. She was apparently experienced in the ways of Africa, indeed she'd been presented to the party as co-leader and driver, so everything seemed in order. They reached their new camp, on a game reserve, that afternoon and Mary suggested they take off on a nature walk. They wouldn't need a guide as there were no predators in the park, but they should take torches anyway as it got dark quickly and they'd be passing beside several water-holes.

At first the party were unsure, but they'd been driving all day and, what the Hell, Mary knew best. Off they went along the path through the bush, past the water-holes, revelling in the distant trumpeting of the elephants and the constant buzz of the wild. For God's sake, they were walking in Africa – it just didn't get any better than this.

Yet it did get a great deal worse. They kept getting lost on the rough path, the terrain got progressively thicker and harsher. Rod began to get tense, realising that they were lost and losing daylight fast. Yet the others paid no heed to his worries – Stella in particular kept wanting to stop and take photos. When he jokingly suggested that he should go in front they all laughed at him. Yet the chuckling became muted by five as darkness fell, and had ceased altogether by 5.30 when it was pitch black. Even with the torches, progress was slow. The path they were following had been washed away, and they found themselves stumbling through a swamp.

By now, Rod was fearing the worst. He knew they had still to pass those water-holes, and that hippos and crocodiles leave the water at night to feed. What they might be feeding on tonight was horribly open to question. Stella recalled that hippos are territorial and might not take kindly to a gang of dopey tourists bumbling through their patch. The party moved on, picking up pace, all the while spurred on by the terrifying sounds emerging from the darkness. They heard splashings in the waters and the snapping of cruel jaws. There were crashings in the bush, twigs snapping only feet away from them. Then the ground began to shake and Rod knew a crocodile wouldn't make that much noise. It was a hippo, and it clearly wanted to give them a piece of its mind. 'It was like Leg it!' remembers Rod 'Oh, Mother of God, leg it, leg it, leg it! Don't even think about it – just GO!'

And leg it they did, in the uproarious and largely pathetic way you'd expect from absolute amateurs. 'We were on our bellies,' recalls Stella, 'We were on our backs, we had mud up to our thighs'. Rod found himself picking people up and hurling them onwards, everyone's heart beating like it was programmed by The Prodigy. Hippos, after all, can cause some nasty, nasty damage. When one bites you, as they say, you stay bitten.

Eventually, the motley band, exhausted and terrified, made it back onto the main road to the camp. Posting two people up front with torches to check for snakes, all they saw on either side of them, as they trudged their weary, wary way home, was eyes. Curious, hungry eyes. Near the camp, they were met by horrified rangers. What did they think they were doing? Didn't anyone tell them about the hippos? No one ventures out there after five, not even rangers, and they've got *guns*.

The next day, one of the rangers took the party (now not the heartiest party, Marty) in a jeep down to the water-holes. There beside the muddy waters were their footprints from the previous evening and in the water, not two metres from the footprints, there was the gaping maw of a gigantic hippopotamus. No one could be in any doubt how close they had come.

Stella and Rod had paid £500 for their safari of a lifetime. African Routes apologised profusely for leading them into the jaws of terror and handed them back £150. The hippo declined to comment.

The one with the big green thing

Goa – halfway up the west coast of India, nestling beside the fabulous Arabian Sea. It's a place of great fame and fantasy. For years now it's been an important eastern stage of the annual hippy trail, where the young, hip and blasted criss-cross the globe in search of the wildest and most spiritually uplifting parties. At Goa there'd be beach parties every night, with Pink Floyd's old sound system making the soft sand shudder to the beat. By paying a little baksheesh to the local lawmen, you could get away with pretty much anything.

But Goa's not just about sand, sex and hi-octane intoxicants. As said, it's beautifully situated amidst one of the greatest and oldest civilisations on the planet. And, as a resort of long experience and high standing it's a wonderful place for a holiday when you're looking for something special.

This was the thinking of Peter and Liz Jordan as they sat at home in windy Whitley Bay, at the north end of the Tyneside conurbation, beside the chilly North Sea. Since they'd been married they'd always taken their holidays in Europe. But with their 25th anniversary approaching, they decided to celebrate in style. They'd try two weeks in Goa, with its swaying palms and ancient temples, its long-horned oxen and exotic foodstuffs. Perusing the Unijet brochure, they picked out the Resorte de Santo Antonio in northern Goa, the hotel appearing to be a shiny bright paragon of classy accommodation, set in the most gorgeous grounds.

But looks can be deceptive, and never more so than in a holiday brochure. The Hotel San Antonio turned out to be in need of more than a little care and attention. And the rooms were in far worse shape than the peeling, yellowing exterior. There were bars on the flaking windows and dirty plywood doors. The curtains had half come away from their rails. In the kitchen the sink was streaked with brown, er, *stuff*. The bed was marked with horribly recognisable stains. Liz sat down and cried, all of her high hopes dashed. The place was revolting.

Immediately, Peter complained to the rep and the couple were moved to a 'better' apartment. It still wasn't great. The toilet didn't flush, and the view from the balcony recalled downtown Beirut. Again Peter approached the rep. This time he was rebuffed with the standard 'You do know you're in India, don't you? What do you expect?'

They certainly didn't expect what happened next. Out

of the drain holes in the bathroom floor, through the windows and doors, from every conceivable nook and crevice came a small army of insects. 'There were baby ants,' said Peter later, 'daddy ants, bullet-head beetles, green things, black things with white spots.' And the ants weren't normal ants, either. They were huge and they bit hard. But even they didn't freak Peter out like the creature that looked like a barnacle stuck to the window. After examining it closely, he plucked up the courage to actually touch it. Instantly eight legs shot out from the sides and it was gone, 'faster than an Exocet'. It gave Peter the fright of his life. Liz, meanwhile, had been careless enough to leave her toothbrush out overnight. She woke to find insects crawling in and out of the bristles. Ugh! 'The only thing missing,' she said, 'was David Bellamy.'

But their ordeal was really only just beginning. Like anyone else on holiday, Peter and Liz liked to sink a few jars more than usual. But here this could not be done. 'You had to have your faculties about you went you went into that room,' explained Liz. For bedtime, when sleep might overtake them and leave the insect interlopers free to creep into any warm orifice they fancied, a strict routine was worked out. First they sprayed themselves from head to toe in repellent. Then they'd put the electric charger on, to fend off the mosquitos. Next they'd check the bed for crawling, glistening guests. Peter would then put on a shirt and trousers before slipping between the sheets, while Liz would tie a further pair of trousers around her head to prevent rogue bugs from scuttling into her hair. Or, worse, her ears.

So it was that Peter Jordan spent the night of his 25th wedding anniversary fully clothed, while his wife had a pair of pants wrapped round her head. Not an ideal way to rekindle those burning passions of yore, you must admit. But this was a minor irritation when compared to the arrival of the Big Green Thing. It happened all of a sudden and without warning. There was Peter making a video of his dear wife to warm his heart in old age when, crawling over her shoulder and down her front, it came. It was huge. It was sickly green. It wore mighty armour. It had big, thick legs, black eyes on stalks, and quivering antennae. It was a grasshopper direct from Chernobyl, a mutant cicada that would have had even Stephen King's bowels emptying into his underpants. On the video footage you can hear Peter say, with typically British understatement, 'Look at the size of *this* bloody thing. It's just … not … *on*'.

The Big Green Thing was the last straw. After a week with no sleep, a week that had been less a relaxing holiday than a crash course in entomology, they decided to leave, a full week before their departure date. The decision made, Peter was a new man, dancing round the pool, singing to the other residents 'I'm going home, I'm going home, I'm go-ing, I am going home'.

In the process of getting out of there, no trouble was too much, no expense too high. They coughed up an extra £414 for their flights and were gone. Compared to this, Whitley Bay seemed like nirvana. It might lack Goa's exotic charms, but at least it wasn't seething with giant bugs. The Jordans were happy once more, and all the more so when Unijet, who claimed to have acted with 'speed and professionalism' when finding them alternative accommodation, offered to repay £650 of their £1070 costs. Considering the number of insects creeping round their apartment in Goa at any given time, this worked out at approximately 10p a leg.

The one with the biblical plague

If the stories in this book teach us anything, it's that when booking a holiday you can take nothing for granted. The package where you get all your food and drink for free? Be careful – there's probably a good reason why that food is free. The hotel that's 'walking distance' from the beach? Watch out – they might mean walking distance for Ranulph Fiennes. And then there are those cheap end-of-season excursions. Now, we're all attracted by the 'cheap' part. Cheap is a good word, we like the cut of its jib. But, in holiday terms, cheap spells danger. It spells rubbish. It spells nightmare. So forget all that nonsense about favourable exchange rates, and spending two weeks in some foreign hotel's presidential suite for £1.50 a night. You buy cheap, you *get* cheap.

This is what happened to Jane and Tim French from Skegness and Jo Davies and her brother, when they booked in at the Pelican Hotel, in the Duni Holiday Village in Bulgaria. They weren't after a five-star holiday (after all, big shoulder pads are *so* passé). Indeed, Jane said that as long as there was a sun-bed for her and a bar for Tim they'd be happy. Jo, meanwhile, just wanted something basic as the trip was to celebrate her brother's 50th birthday and he'd always wanted to see Bulgaria. The seeing was the main thing. Both parties had been attracted by the price – £287 each for two weeks – as the brochure made the hotel out to be worth far more. It had open-air dining facilities, barbecues, a wine cellar and a nightclub. It was just two hundred metres from a Black Sea beach, it had an outdoor sports centre and, so the brochure had it, 'the pool area is particularly pleasant'.

They had a feeling something was up as soon as they arrived. A group of other tourists approached them and said, 'Welcome to Stalag 13. We're escaping on Wednesday, how long have *you* got to do?' With their fabulously warped sense of humour, the Brits can be so hard to suss. Was this a wind-up or a warning? Undaunted, they decided to inspect their new surroundings. First, the outdoor sports centre.

It wasn't what they'd expected. Rather than a gleaming expanse of virgin Astroturf filled with happy holidaymakers batting, booting and slam-dunking plastic balls, they found a miserable span of grey concrete. There were no people anywhere, everything was broken. There was a big open hole in the ground, fifteen feet deep. On the wire-enclosed concrete five-a-side pitch, the goalposts were snapped and slumped, as if they'd suffered the jubilant, boozy aftermath of a Scottish victory over England. Then there was the pool, sullied with leaves and branches. The water was clear, but that only served to reveal how filthy the bottom was. Oddly, the pool was packed. But not with people. Flitting across this man-made pond and stretching out their webbed fingers and toes to stick to the sides, were frogs, hundreds of frogs. It was an amazing display of amphibious life, a French restaurateur's wet dream.

Strolling back to the hotel, they approached the second pool, the one that had looked so enticing in the brochure. This was more like it. Nicely tiled and surrounded by sun-loungers and potted palms, it looked the ideal spot for a couple of weeks of unbridled sloth. Then, still some distance from the water, they noticed something strange. A young child was running around the pool, occasionally dipping his hand in but mostly just staring into the water. He seemed thoroughly disinclined to actually jump in. They immediately jumped to the obvious conclusion. And they were right. When they reached the pool they discovered that it too was brimful of batrachians – it was frog heaven. They couldn't believe it.

Had they been fans of religious shockers like *The Omen* and *The Seventh Sign*, they might at this point have asked themselves a serious question. Was it possible that the Hotel Pelican had somehow brought God's wrath down upon itself? The sports centre *was* pretty rough. Had the swimming pool recently been turned to blood? Because that's how it usually goes. First the blood, then the frogs. After that the dust turns into lice, then come the flies, and the pestilence that strikes down all the animals. Then everyone gets boils, locusts cover the land and it all goes dark. If things still don't get sorted out, it's ta-ta to everyone's first-born. Had the families French and Davies consulted their bibles, they might have been more concerned than bemused.

But the holidaymakers were concentrating on something other than potential plagues. For on the other side of the pool was the most extraordinary sight. Stooping low over the side to lap up the water were two cows. Cows! Apparently cattle came there to drink all the time. Not only would this make one a tad suspicious about the amount of cleansing chlorine in the water, but all those frogs and oxen made a screaming mockery of the swimming experience. When you're powering through the water, eating up the lengths, you feel strong, athletic,

Olympian. You're Mark Spitz, not Dr Dolittle, for Christ's sake!

For the families it just kept getting worse. There was a very definite end-of-season feeling about the place. Indeed, judging from the state of the rooms, the season had ended several years before. They were filthy, so bad that people ended up cleaning the bathrooms themselves. Down on the beach, the plethora of parasols and waterside tables that had stood out so brightly in the brochure had all been packed away.

This really wasn't on. At the meeting with the holiday rep vociferous complaints were made. The rep had the same justification for everything – 'It's Bulgaria, it's Bulgaria'. Nothing could be done. When they watched men come with little barrows and take away the potted palms from beside the pool – the palms, the last remaining luxury item – they knew the game was up. They sat back and gloomily waited to leave. Stalag 13, indeed. The beaches of Skegness now seemed appetising in the extreme.

Having, as mentioned, paid £287 each to endure the Hotel Pelican, they naturally demanded compensation. The £100 each they were offered would not be enough. There had been no frogs in the brochure, and no cows either. Yet again someone was suffering the end-of-season cheap package blues. So beware, or you too will find yourself doing the backstroke in a big cows' trough.

The one with all the flies

Why is it that we all hate flies? After all, we don't despise other insects that are far uglier and more dangerous. We all marvel at the intimidating armour of the stag beetle, and applaud its clumsy efforts at flight. We chuckle at the bumblebee and wonder why he doesn't make two trips, rather than weigh himself down so foolishly. We can even tolerate locusts, as long as there's only one and it does its best to pretend it's a grasshopper.

But flies? No way. At the slightest hint of that annoying buzz, ordinarily sensitive and kind people will seize the nearest periodical, roll it into a vicious truncheon and race about the room, hacking at the walls and leaping to wallop the ceiling. So keen are they to take the life of a fellow creature, they care not if they knock over a few vases or crack a few window panes.

We all do it. But why? Is it because we think all flies are on a mission to trample over sticky-fresh dog-doo before clambering around the lip of our glass of lemonade? Yes, it is. Is it because we're revolted by the fact that, to eat their food, flies must first vomit acid all over it and then suck up the soup? Yes, it is. Is it because when a fly starts buzzing around you it will never, ever, ever stop? Yes, it is. We hate the fly's relentlessness. On and on it goes, the sound rising and falling as it careers about the room. Then silence. Thank God, it's gone.

There are many reasons to hate flies, but this is the main one. They *insist* upon it. And here's another theory. We kill flies in revenge. Not for habitually vomiting near us, or for making us eat fresh dog-doo. No, ours is a vendetta of long standing, and it stems from when we were in the cradle. Of course, none of us can remember those long, dull days when there was nothing to look forward to but fake milk and the occasional terrifying appearance of a giant head with halitosis. But there is one thing we can be sure we all shared as an experience – at some point there must have been a fly. It probably smeared dog-doo on your innocent face, maybe vomited onto your sweet-smelling skin. It definitely buzzed – that's what they do. And if it started buzzing, it *kept* buzzing. It buzzed and it buzzed and it nearly crawled in your little ear, and there was nothing you could do with your pudgy arms and tiny fingers to stop it. All you could do was scream your impotent rage into its black, multi-faceted eyes as it did exactly what it wanted with you. In rap-speak, you were a fly's bitch. And, subconsciously, you have not forgotten.

As said, we can't remember this, but it must have happened. As the Americans say – do the math. There's trillions of flies. You can't escape them, especially not if you haven't learned to walk yet. And that's why flies send us mad. We're simply doing what we were powerless to do all those years ago. It's payback time, you buzzing bastards!

Imagine then the horror and frustration of Matthew, Annabel and their partners when they booked a holiday at the Hotel Agua Marina, otherwise known as Club Flamingo, in Melonar in southern Spain. It should have been great. The hotel was one of several white blocks squatting beside the bright blue Mediterranean and the amenities were fine. There were four bars, two pools and three pool-side bars. There was a beautiful beach for jetskiing, canoeing and windsurfing. There were all-you-can-eat buffets for breakfast, lunch and dinner, and a pizzeria. Despite the building work in the lobby and the graffiti scrawled on the lifts, the couples were very impressed with their surroundings.

Sadly, the guests weren't the only ones enjoying the hotel's hospitality. Down by the pools, thousands of flies congregated, greedily sucking up any sweetness they could find. The bars were alive with them, they were all over the walls, the floors and the counters. If you went into the water, you'd come back to find them lined up around the rim of your glass, or performing a panicked backstroke in your drink. Everyone was slapping themselves continually on the legs, the arms, the neck and the face. You could never find peace for more than a few seconds at a time. Matthew, a fisherman, reckoned he didn't think there'd be more flies at a maggot farm. It really was that bad.

One of the problems was the hotel's refuse procedures. The insects were clearly encouraged by the unemptied bins rammed with cans, half-eaten food and plastic glasses. The tables were seldom cleared, with the remains of fruity cocktails often being left out all night. Annabel complained to the resort manager, but was told in no uncertain terms that the hotel was 'perfectly acceptable'. After three days in this buzzing purgatory, she paid for the last seat on an outgoing aircraft and went home. Matthew and the others were not so lucky. They were forced to slap themselves raw for the rest of their two weeks.

Each couple had paid £1274 for their fly-ridden vacation. Thankfully, First Choice recognised their disappointment and granted them a full refund, as well as a further £50 as a goodwill gesture. They also paid Annabel's extra flight costs. They said they would be fully investigating the situation at the Hotel Agua Marina. It is to be hoped that the report recommended the introduction of several battalions of the Spanish military, armed to the teeth with rolled-up copies of the *Melanor Times*. *That*'d sort 'em out.

The one with the smoky bar

We may hate flies, but we *fear* mosquitos. We all recall the sharp pain as one of them stabs its syringe of a nose through our skin and starts guzzling on our life-blood. Perhaps even worse is the hard, itching lump that rises over the wound, refusing to deflate for weeks. Some of us have even had the misfortune to contract malaria from the droning devils. Apparently, tonic water's good for that. The large gin is optional.

Pete and Betty Russell had not been told of any mosquito problem when they booked a Hayes and Jarvis holiday on Cayo Largo, Cuba. If the brochure had mentioned it, they said later, they'd have gone tooled up with repellent and one of those neat electronic killers. But it hadn't, and they didn't, and consequently they were slowly being eaten alive.

Yet, amazingly, the Russells weren't as troubled by the insects as they were by the locals' attempts at mosquito genocide. The video footage of this is really quite extraordinary. There are the guests in the hotel bar. It's a nice bar, more of a cocktail lounge, really, and everyone is dressed in casual but smart evening-wear. They're having an enviably classy good time. Then, looking over the happy people to the reception area, we see a huge billow of smoke burst through the open glass doors, as if a building opposite had collapsed. But there's no sound of crashing masonry, just the heavy grind of a big machine. The cloud grows and thickens, making reception disappear. Then it rolls over the wooden division and into the bar. People quickly cover their mouths and their drinks as they're totally enveloped. More smoke pours through the open window above the rows of spirits. Visibility is down to two feet. Everyone appears in ghostly silhouette – it's like TV news coverage of some desert war.

And no one's complaining. Apparently, it happened every night and had actually become a social function. People wanted to see how thick it would get tonight, how long it would last. It was fun, but it was also a tad disturbing. Pete asked his rep what it was and was told it was insecticide. And what chemicals were in it, exactly? Oh, er, no one was quite sure.

It wasn't that the insecticide made you feel ill, just a little uncomfortable. But the Russells, as Pete quite rightly pointed out, had gone on holiday to relax, not to be fumigated nightly. They'd paid £2256 and the brochure had mentioned neither the biting bugs nor the unwanted cloud-baths. Hayes and Jarvis, though, would give no compensation. They were sorry the holiday had been marred, but the insecticide had met all the requirements of the Cuban Ministry of Health. No one made a claim of behalf of the dead mosquitos.

The one with all the hamsters

Due to the millions of extra tourists travelling abroad each year, in general operators haven't made too many improvements to their services. What they *have* improved, though, is the excuses they use to avoid paying compensation for unsatisfactory holidays. Some are quite thrilling in their devious innovation. Indeed, the one that features in the following tale is so hilariously witty, so daring in its brazen invention, it really deserves an award.

This is not, of course, to belittle the suffering of Caroline and Christina Denning. Through Airtours, they booked a corker of a holiday, a trip to the Maldives, a spectacularly exotic group of islands set in the Indian Ocean. Just one glimpse at their video footage shows that this is a paradise of white sands, blue seas and gently swaying palm trees. It seemed they had most certainly landed on their feet.

But they didn't think that when something *else* landed on their feet. As dusk fell and they made their way to the restaurant for their evening meal, they both felt something scamper across their sandals. Naturally fearful, they asked each other the same questions. Did you see that? Was that a rat? It *was* furry.

Bravely investigating, they began to poke around amongst the wide green leaves of the undergrowth and, sure enough, out jumped a rat, quickly scurrying away. Then they spotted another. And another. And then they realised that this tropical woodland was teeming with them, they were actually falling out of the trees. It was like the appalling finale of Robert Southey's grim but exciting morality poem 'Bishop Hatto' – the rats were *everywhere*.

The Dennings span about and rushed on to the restaurant. Yet even here they were not safe from the rampaging vermin. Before long there was a horrified squawk as someone spotted a furry interloper. The staff chased the unwelcome visitor out, but the rat's devil-may-care entrance had affected Caroline and Christina deeply. From now on, they would get little sleep. Instead they'd lie awake, listening to the scurrying and the scratching outside their door, knowing full well what it was, and imagining what it wanted to do.

The reason for the infestation was easily discovered. Just a short way inland, away from the gorgeous beach, the women discovered a very different world, a world of rubbish tips among the trees, with trash scattered everywhere. It was an obvious breeding ground, absolutely horrible.

On her return home to Scotland, Caroline wrote an angry letter of complaint to Airtours. And here appears that classic excuse. Airtours wrote back telling her that they weren't rats, they were ... wait for it ... Maldivan Palm Hamsters. Isn't that fantastic? That's better than people in south London claiming they live in St Reatham.

Caroline was not to be fobbed off like that. Her next letter was to Edinburgh Zoo, asking if they could give her any information about the Maldivan Palm Hamster. They were intrigued. They didn't have one of those. Indeed, they'd never even heard of it. Their pride chipped and interest piqued, research officers including Kristian Andersen scoured their reference books and all relevant

Internet sites. They found nothing. Returning to Caroline, they asked for further description of the creature. She said simply, 'It's got a six-inch tail and looks like a rat'.

Now a more rigorous academic inquiry began. The research operators trawled through the wildlife directories of many countries, they checked endangered species lists. They found nothing. In desperation they called Caroline in to the zoo to examine the animals they had and the pictures they'd found. Again there was no result. There were no other avenues to explore, they had no choice. They had to conclude that the Maldivan Palm Hamster looked like a rat because it *was* a rat.

Utterly vindicated, Caroline wrote once more to Airtours. The game was up. Airtours replied by saying there'd been a misunderstanding. It seemed the local Maldivan staff had taken to calling the rats by a humorous name and this had caused confusion. They were sorry for their 'inappropriate use of the local nickname' and would be happy to refund £450 of the Dennings' £2252 costs. Beyond this, they would be looking into the refuse situation and reprimanding the hoteliers for their inadequate pest control.

It's a shame, in a way. The notion of cuddly hamsters living in palm trees is an appealing one. And not just to us. If you ever wondered what hamsters dream of during their long days trapped in a dusty cage and running insanely on a wire wheel, this is probably it. Poor little blighters.

The one with the bitten head

Many of us have children, and we know what a drain they can be, both on your finances and your mental health. We all need an occasional break from their relentless and usually unreasonable demands. Trouble is, we're not allowed to leave them at home while we go on holiday. Or put them in kennels (where most of them belong). It's not a satisfactory situation, but it's the law. Consequently parents never get to really relax, not ever.

Jacob Guy and Marion Little thought they'd found a solution to this perennial problem when they booked an Airtours trip to Spain with their two young girls. The package offered a free children's club with all manner of excursions and activities. *Fantastic*, they thought, the kids will play and maybe learn things and we'll have some time to ourselves. Of course they assumed that all the activities would be safe, and paid no heed to the mention of sharks in the brochure. After all, beside the shark-infested paragraph was a cute and cuddly cartoon shark with a big smile on its face. *Aaah*, lovely little shark.

The more paranoid among us might have grown suspicious at a kids' trip to the local zoo. *Would* there be sharks? Because if anyone's crazy enough to keep sharks they'll probably have grizzly bears and Bengal tigers and black mambas roaming around, too. Anyone keeping a shark clearly has no sense of danger or decorum. But Jacob and Marion, a decent couple with normal perceptions, weren't paranoid. They thought their children would be safe at the zoo. Only people who climb into the cage to take a close-up shot of Mr Lion get hurt at the zoo, don't they?

So off the two girls went. At the zoo they were told all the usual safety rules. Don't put your fingers through the wire cages, don't feed yourself to Mr Lion etc etc. They were having a great time. They saw the camels, the elephants, the monkeys, the parrots, all the fangs and plumages a child's heart could desire. And then came the crocodile pit. This, as you can imagine, was a deep hole with steep sloping sides. At the bottom, basking in the sun with their cruel mouths half-open and their evil eyes flickering, were the crocodiles. Several of them were all wound up in a grotesque little heap, probably seeking some familial comfort, as everyone else hates them.

Intrigued by these monsters, little Clare leant over the low wall surrounding the pit to take photos. It was lucky she was trying to take pictures, for her camera may well have saved her life. Before she could focus through the viewfinder, one of the crocodiles in the seemingly docile heap span round, surged up the steep slope and snapped its jaws shut on her. For a few seconds, it had her by the hair then, gravity be praised, it slipped back down to join its beastly brothers once more. Clare recognised what had happened. She was appalled to find that she had *crocodile spit* in her hair. And then she realised that she was bleeding.

The reps found Jacob and Marion very quickly. Clare's had a little accident at the zoo, they said, she's been bitten. Bitten by what, the parents asked – a parrot? A goat? A monkey? No, came the terrifying reply, it was a crocodile.

What thoughts would go through your head if someone told you that? They were absolutely horrified, particularly Jacob who'd recently seen a nature programme on crocodiles. He'd seen them attack other creatures, much bigger creatures than Clare. And he knew that crocodiles like to bring their prey down by the head. In exactly what state would they find their poor little girl?

Thankfully, all she required was several stitches in a deep cut beside her left eyebrow. That camera had stopped those jaws from closing around her face and dragging her down into the pit. She had been inches from a dreadful fate.

Naturally, Jacob and Marion were shocked, angry and relieved all at once. This should never have occurred when their child was in the care of a responsible company. On their return home, they requested compensation from Airtours. They had, after all, paid £1235 for this bad dream. Airtours informed them that they'd cancelled all zoo trips forthwith and had ordered a complete review of their excursion programme worldwide. They gave the parents a whopping £18 – the price of the trip to the zoo.

The one with the hairy monster

One of the main reasons people are willing to pay the criminal sums charged for house surveys is that they fear damp. Damp will creep through a place, wrecking its look and then its structure. Damp slowly destroys everything in its path. For home-owners it's a nightmare.

For mould, though, damp is a wet dream. Mark and Louise Sanders discovered this when they took cheap accommodation in Greece, along with their teenage son. Because of the low price they'd expected their rooms to be basic. But no one could have been prepared for what they witnessed when they first flicked the light switch.

Over in the back of the room, in the left corner, a pipe had clearly been boxed in and concealed. Whether this had made it angry, no one knows, but it had certainly spluttered water everywhere. And where the water went, so appeared the mould. Yet this was no ordinary mould culture. It wasn't like you find on old bread or on a pair of wet trainers you've left too long in the garage. This was a gathering of mould to outdo all others. It was the Glastonbury Festival of the mould world.

It started, Mark recalled, at the ceiling, across which it spread like an evil black pool. Then, as it descended the wall, it turned to a deep brown, then ripened into a dull orange before brightening into a glaring yellow. By the time it reached the floor, it was green with long hairs growing from it. It was five feet across and seven and a half tall and it looked, Mark later laughed, as if it were alive, as if it could move, as if it were waiting to grab you.

Sounds silly, doesn't it? But stop for a second and imagine just what it would be like to be grabbed by mould. What if you were loitering by a wall, for whatever reason, and it suddenly dropped over you like a slimy sheet, flattening you to the wall, moulding itself to your contours and rendering your limbs immovable. Feel how it blocks your nose with its grim stench, sticks to your lips, forces its way over your tongue and oozes down your throat. It's tightening its grip, you can't breathe ... oh, God! When mould attacks, you really don't want to be there.

Anyway, the Sanders' mould turned out not be predatory. But it was persistent. Two days after they made their first complaint, a man came round with a brush and a bucket of whitewash, gave the offending culture a right pasting and made the room look spick and span once more.

Well, the mould wasn't having *that*. By the next day it was back with a vengeance. If anything, its varied hues were more vivid than before. They complained again, and back came the man with the brush. This time he gave it a coat so thick and liberal Howard Hodgkin would have approved. But come the weekend the multicoloured fungus had returned.

By now the enormous and vibrant damp patch had for

the Sanders become a major talking-point, and a huge joke. On a trip to an ancient monastery, Mark told the other visitors, 'Our wall's worse than that. You ought to come and see our wall'. He wasn't wrong. Their wall *was* worse, and every time they had a shower or pulled the flush in the bathroom above, it got worse still. Also, the smell was now all-pervading. You know that smell. It's not the deep, earthy whiff of woodland moss, it's the smell of, well, the *grave*. No one likes that smell. It makes us think that we're actually *not* going to be the first person to live forever.

After the monastery trip, the mould began to receive visitors of its own. So often did the Sanders mention their unwanted guest that others were intrigued. Every day more people came round to see what all the fuss was about, and its fame grew across the complex and beyond. One night there were twelve of them. The Sanders noted that on one boat excursion there were fewer people than had come to view their mould.

By the end of their stay, it had almost become part of the family. Indeed all three of the Sanders caught themselves saying 'Bye, wall' as they left. It had been fun – but of course it was also utterly outrageous. They were quite rightly refunded £450 of the £927 they'd spent. Mouldy old dough, indeed.

3 Danger! Danger!

The chances of anything going badly wrong during your holiday are very low. But they are there. And we're not talking about minor pains here, like getting an electric shock off your door-handle or having your swimming costume slide off as you pull yourself out of the pool. We're talking about violence, terror and the reckless endangerment of life. The characters in the following set of stories have suffered a crazy variety of problems. Some of them may have crossed your mind as possibilities, others certainly won't have. Read on, to see just how bad it gets.

The one with the psycho landlord

Corfu: a beautiful island sitting in the Ionian Sea, by the Strait of Otranto, just to the west of Greece. The place has everything for the family holiday. Wonderful weather and a spectacular coastline of shining white rock dropping into the azure ocean. On Corfu, you can't help but relax as the stress is warmed from your bones and you feel yourself at one with nature and the magnificent history of the area. Wasn't it across these very waters that the priestess Io swam, after she'd been turned into a heifer by the jealous goddess Juno? They were right sods, those gods.

Well, relaxation was exactly what Pete Greenhough and his family needed, a break in the so-called Land of Smiles. So, through Thomson, they booked themselves into the Spiros Pool Bar, a pretty little complex with all the necessities and plenty more. What the brochure didn't mention, though, was that across the road lay Yannis Village, another apartment complex boasting a 'free swimming pool, super jacuzzi, snack bar, mini-market, public telephone, children's playground, satellite TV'. It also boasted Telis, the genial host, said to arrange 'entertainment which provides a lively, friendly atmosphere'. Just how lively and friendly the Greenhoughs were soon to find out.

The first night they were assailed by your average disco music. Not easy to sleep through, that. The second night brought karaoke, and the thoroughly unedifying sound of very drunk people pretending to be Gloria Gaynor. Bound to keep you awake. Then, as Pete remembers it, on the third or fourth night, came the crunch. About four in the morning, the Yannis bar, already noisy, burst into a rousing rendition (well, it certainly roused everyone who wasn't already awake) of Roy 'Chubby' Brown's violent dismantling of Smokie's 'Living Next Door To Alice'. You know the words to that one. At least seven of them, anyway.

This was the last straw for Pete. He had kids there, for God's sake. He crossed over from the Spiros to the Yannis bar, saw Telis playing his affable landlord role to the hilt and, through the din of music, laughter and chinking bottles and glasses, shouted something along the lines of 'Excuse me, can I have a word with you about the noise?' Telis looked around at him, measured him up and then took off down to the other end of the bar at high speed. It wasn't that he was cowed by Pete's appearance. Rather, as he reached the entrance to the kitchen, he snatched up a large knife and turned to face his unwelcome inquisitor, shaking one fist at him in an impressively menacing manner, and clutching the blade in the other, all the while yelling vitriolic abuse. Pete recalls the gist being 'You come on my property again, I kill you! I kill you!' And then he started coming down the bar. Pete took off. Not bothering with the path leading to the road and the Spiros, he went directly over the nearest wall.

Pete claims he wrote to Sun World about this incident with the not-so-genial Telis. They say they have no record of any such letter. Suffice to say nothing was done and the next year Jim Hunt, Mandy Jones and their one-year-old son Ross arrived on Corfu, this time actually booked into Telis's Yannis apartment complex. At first all went well. In fact, it was great. They soon enjoyed a drink in the Yannis bar and Telis was thoroughly charming, all smiles and warm handshakes. What a guy. They could really get to like it around here.

Until night fell, that is. As had happened the year before, the noise from the bar was excruciating. Jim noticed that once most people had gone to bed, a hard-core clique of drinkers, maybe ten or twelve, plus Telis himself, would continue on till four or five in the morning, loudly singing, swearing and telling jokes. It was all a bit much, it left a bad taste in the mouth. Jim and Mandy took to spending more and more time at the Spiros complex across the road.

No harm in that, eh? Apparently there was. One day Jim was returning to his apartment, holding a half-eaten ice cream. As he passed the bar Telis pounced with an aggressive 'Oi! We sell ice creams here!' Thinking this was an ideal situation to explain his feelings about the noise at night, Jim entered the bar and, before he had a chance to open his mouth, his genial host flipped out. 'He called me everything,' recalled Jim later, 'from a pig to a dog. His language was unreal . . . over an *ice cream.*' Suddenly, Telis leant forward over the bar and tried to grab his new-found enemy. Jim stepped back, and left.

But it wasn't over yet. A few days later, Jim was walking around the pool with little Ross on his shoulders when he passed Telis. The landlord said nothing, but his expression made Jim think he was just about to. Suddenly, Telis burst into a hail of abuse, Jim turned to face him and was punched right in the face. Telis's next blow was lower, it struck Jim on the chest and simultaneously knocked Ross backwards such that he was hanging over his father's back, over the water, with Jim gripping his leg in one hand. If this wasn't discomfiting enough, with the other hand he was trying to ward off the blows that the incensed Telis was now raining down on him.

Across the pool, Mandy saw events unfold and her baby son thus endangered. Screaming for Telis to stop she raced round to Jim and grabbed Ross before he fell. Now with both arms free, you'd think Jim would have a chance to defend his corner. No chance. For also watching the mêlée was Telis's father, who quickly locked Jim in a bear-hug from behind, allowing his son, now shrieking with rage, to paste him some more. Ref-er-*ee*!

And, once the pasting was over, it got even *worse*. Jim and Mandy were given fifteen minutes to pack up and get off the site. In fact, they didn't even have to pack. While Jim was being unceremoniously tossed through the gates, Mandy sat crying on her bed, watching all their possessions being stuffed violently into their bags. The full quarter of an hour was not required.

Complaining to Sun World, Jim and Mandy were told that Telis had every right to ask them to leave his property. It must have been a personal dispute, none of their business. As for the noise, well, only three people had complained last year. How bad could it be? As for Telis, he claimed he pushed Jim but didn't hit him. He said he was severely provoked. And, really, haven't all of us, at some time or another, been driven to the edge of violence by the sight of a man eating an ice cream? And if he were then to have the unmitigated gall to walk past us with a child sitting on his shoulders, could any one of us control our spiralling rage? Wouldn't you feel compelled, by all that is right, just and moral, to batter him about the face while your dad held his arms? Exactly ...

So Jim Hunt was abused, threatened and beaten. His partner was terrified and his son placed in severe danger of falling head-first onto the pool-side, even onto the pool's stone edge. And he had no recourse at all. You can be sure he'll not be forgetting his Holiday in Hades in a hurry.

The one with all the smoke

As our mammonite government slips further in thrall to Brussels (aside from the occasional unsanctioned attack on Middle Eastern countries), safety regulations in Britain are now strict beyond the call of rhyme or reason. We assume that someone somewhere is shielding us from every potential danger, or at the very least standing guard ready to sue the butt off anyone who causes us harm.

This almost entirely unfounded confidence in our

'superiors' can get us into terrible trouble when we leave this sceptred isle. For not only do different countries have the temerity to speak different languages, eat different foods and worship different gods, they also have different ideas as to what constitutes safety. Paul and Cheryl Lloyd discovered this for themselves, as did Susan Chappell and Pat Rice when Kwik Travel booked them cheap holidays at the Corres Del Sol apartments on Tenerife.

Their apartments were, it must be admitted, very nice. The Lloyds in particular were pleased as punch to be fifteen storeys up with such a wonderful view of the resort. They spent their first evening sampling the delights of Tenerife's famous night-life, a flashing neon wonderland of bars, clubs and restaurants, all of them packed with glowing happy faces.

But things changed rapidly. Having taken a fairly early night so as to refresh themselves for a blissful tomorrow, they were awoken at six in the morning by a loud banging. Paul Lloyd assumed it was someone drunkenly kicking a door open, or hammering for admittance having mislaid the key. He got out of bed and opened his own door, to check out what was going on. He shut the door a great deal quicker than he opened it.

From the expression on his face, Cheryl knew that something was desperately wrong. Paul had seen that the corridor was filled with billowing black smoke, almost obscuring a deep red glow. He could tell that the fire was blocking their way out and that, from the increasing heat, it was close and getting closer still. Suddenly, they heard a woman's terrified scream. The smell was appalling, like the sickening stench of burning tyres and they realised from the poisoned burning in their noses, throats and lungs that smoke was entering the room.

Sensibly, they grabbed their towels and the sheets from the bed and soaked them in the bath, before using them to line the door. Only now did they think of phoning for help, and only now did they discover that there was no phone. Paul ran to the window. There were no balconies to allow a sideways clamber to safety. Looking upwards he saw that there was no way up to the roof. There was no escape. Leaning out of the window, they saw the people milling far below, ant-sized and out of earshot. They yelled down anyway – 'Fire! Help! Fire!' – and in frustrating return a group of cheery holiday-makers waved backed, shouting 'Ole! Ole!'

But the Lloyds weren't waving, they were drowning in smoke. Forced to wait for help to arrive, help that might not ever come, they began to pray for their lives. Choking now, they had to lean out of the window to breathe. Next door, Pat Rice was coming to a decision. With a horror of burning to death, she made up her mind that, when the fire entered the room, she would ease herself out of the window and, at the last possible moment, when the flames drew near and all hope was extinguished, she would jump.

After forty-five dreadful minutes, long enough for their lives to flash past their eyes in slow, cruel detail, they heard a commotion out in the corridor. Cheryl Lloyd risked opening the door to see shadowy figures carrying torches emerge from the clouds of dense black smoke. They were security guards. Throwing the wet sheets around the terrified guests, they escorted them through the smoke and down fifteen flights of stairs to fresh air and freedom.

The rescued tourists were profoundly relieved but soon angry. With the corridor outside their room entirely gutted by the fire, they discovered that, though there were extinguishers on the walls of the corridor (unreachable, as it had turned out), there were no smoke or fire alarms, and no sprinkler systems in place. Furthermore, there were no notices in the rooms imparting the safest course of action in the event of a problem.

Holiday Which? annually inspects hundreds of apartments and hotels, and they report that almost one third fail to meet even the most basic standards of fire safety. Kwik Travel informed Susan Chappell and Pat Rice that the Corres Del Sol apartments were in fact licensed to an appropriate standard by the Spanish authorities, yet nevertheless gave them a full refund on their holiday.

What they had missed, of course, was some jumped-up Little Hitler of a security guard, flouncing about in an ill-fitting uniform, testing the alarms at inconvenient times of the morning and forcing all the guests to learn the safety notices off-by-heart before they'd unpacked their bags. They had flown far away from the diabolical pettiness of Britain's lesser officials and nearly paid a terrible price. One hopes they remember this fact the next time they're severely admonished for daring to breathe the air when passing through a First Class carriage on the train.

The one with the stolen child

It's important to remember that, when we travel abroad on holiday, we're not just leaving our cares and troubles behind. We're not simply saying adieu to the wind and the rain and the bumper Sunday edition of *EastEnders*. We're also abandoning a system we know and understand. A system that, in general, looks after us. We're walking away from the police, the legal system and many of the rights that we ordinarily take for granted.

On holiday, people tend to feel that they're still protected. They've paid their insurance (hopefully after reading the small print very, very closely) and, hey, if things go wrong there's always that nice rep they met at the welcome meeting. But the rep is not charged with looking after you outside the very narrow boundaries of your holiday package. They have very little responsibility for your well-being. You may have to turn to the police and there is no guarantee whatsoever that they'll be sympathetic to your cause. After all, it's near certain that most of their problems are caused by holidaymakers just like you.

Neil and Jackie Matheson had their eyes brutally opened when they took their young son and daughter off on an Airtours holiday to Ibiza. Their break had started brilliantly. The kids had loved sloshing about in the pool in their little water-wings. They'd screamed with delight while riding the mini-fire engine and the other fairground attractions. They were, in contemporary parlance, up for it.

Neil and Jackie were enjoying it, too. Indeed, the only drawback as far as they could tell was the street traders. Dressed in sombreros and Newcastle United shirts, they were a constant pest, always tapping you on the shoulder, trying to persuade you to buy a bracelet, or pair of sunglasses, or something, from the trays of tat they carried around. They were everywhere – on the beach, in the cafés, on the streets, all over the complex. A right pain. But things could be so much worse, right? Determined not to get uptight, the Mathesons concentrated instead on their own good time.

One night, the family went out for a meal with some new friends they'd made, and afterwards they invited them back to the complex. They were having a good old laugh, all performing a hilarious flamenco, kids and adults together. Neil was sitting down, having recently undergone a knee operation, and he noticed his little son Connor totter down the hall to the toilet.

In the midst of all the fun Lorraine, one of their new friends, looked down off the balcony and saw one of the street sellers, garbed in the standard stripey shirt, coming out of the complex and moving off towards the beach. But he wasn't on his own. To her dismay, she noticed that against his shoulder he was holding little Connor Matheson.

Leaping up, and pausing only to inform the boy's parents, she took off after the kidnapper, Neil following as quickly as his leg would allow. Lorraine forced herself to go faster and faster, keenly aware that the man could so easily slip out of sight in the gathering night. Luckily, he was slowed by his infant burden and she caught up with him just as he moved onto the beach. 'That's not your son,' she said. 'You don't take other people's children.' He looked straight back at her with a mystified and mystifying expression. 'Oh, God,' she thought, 'what is he going to do?' Yet, despite her fear, she took Connor from the man's arms, stood him on the sand and began to walk away. Connor, evidently petrified, clung to her with all his useless might. She expected the worst, but the man made no effort to reclaim his stolen prize.

Back at the complex, Jackie asked her frightened boy where the man had taken him from – had he strayed outside? The answer stunned them all, Connor replying, 'The man came in the toilet and took me out of the toilet, mummy'. With their security breached so easily and almost disastrously, the Mathesons were deeply upset. By now all the children were crying, there was an air of panic to the party. Neil tried to call Airtours back in London but couldn't get through. They tried to contact their rep, Leanne, but their efforts again proved fruitless. It was no good. They'd have to wait until tomorrow.

Early the next day, Jackie went looking for Leanne. Unsuccessful once more, she went to reception to leave a message telling the rep to come to their room immediately upon her return. When the receptionist asked what it concerned, Jackie explained that her child had been snatched the night before. The receptionist seemed to think it was a joke. Jackie did not take this well, now *demanding* that the message be passed on.

When the rep arrived at their room, Jackie explained the situation again. And again she was horrified when Leanne, too, seemed to think it was a joke. Really, said the rep, didn't they think it might have been some kind of prank? Try as they might, they could not convince her to take it seriously.

On their return to the UK, the Mathesons wrote to Airtours complaining about the incident and the way it was dealt with (or, more accurately, *not* dealt with). Airtours wrote back, apologising for their distress, but adding that it *could* have been some sort of joke. Nevertheless, they repaid the family £850 of the £1700 they'd spent on their holiday. Airtours also assured them that street sellers were now banned from the complex. Yet

Lorraine, who stayed one week longer than Neil and Jackie, saw no change in policy and, when a *Holidays from Hell* camera crew turned up a few weeks later, there were still hawkers in the cafés.

Connor, meanwhile, had become a clingy child where before he'd been far more confident. He wasn't sleeping well and, for the first time, was demanding that the light be left on in his bedroom. His feelings of security had been taken from him so swiftly. They would be much harder to replace.

The one with the collapsing hotel

Love, as the immortal bard once put it, is a many splendour'd thing. Sweet and delicate, it demands our utmost attention, lest it wither away or simply scarper. There are those among us, of a more poetical bent, who believe the government should hand grants out to young couples. This would serve not only as a long-overdue national tribute to Cupid and Aphrodite, but also permit the couples' love to flourish in a stress-free environment. Thus they would be bound more tightly together and, hopefully, never become a drain on the judicial system by splitting up and fighting a bitter custody battle over the juicer.

Adam and Jenny were a young couple with a sensible attitude towards their relationship. This was why they spent

£1365 on a romantic week's break at the Hotel Picafort Park on Mallorca. They wanted high-quality time together in high-quality surroundings and, for a while at least, that's just what they got. The hotel was lovely. The balcony had a life-affirming view out over the sparkling sea. They spent many hours relaxing by and in the luxurious pool, being photographed sitting happily astride a big stone seal and standing between the jaws of a huge dragon's head.

There are those who believe it to be extremely foolish to mock even an effigy of the dragon, and they would nod their heads sagely (and very irritatingly) were they to hear what happened next. Returning to their room, Adam and Jenny found that the air-conditioning machine wasn't working any more. Putting it down to the rapidly increasing temperature, they ignored it, just as they ignored the cracks they now noticed in the corners of the walls and around the patio doors. They must have been there all along – they just hadn't noticed in the excitement of their arrival.

But more strange events began to occur. The radio kept turning on for no reason at all. They were disturbed by numerous sudden banging noises, one particular thud in the night convincing Jenny that Adam had fallen out of bed. Then there was a loud crash from the bathroom. There was no damage, nothing had fallen, but the shower became a slow trickle.

That night, leaving the room, Adam tried to close the door behind them but found that it was sticking against the frame. Odd – it hadn't done that before. Then, while trying to pull it to, they noticed a large sideways crack in the wall between their door and their neighbour's, a crack so big Jenny could fit her little finger into it. Had they not seen that either? Deciding to forget about it for now, they went down to the hotel restaurant and enjoyed a peaceful and romantic dinner for two.

Once they'd finished their meal, rather than going out on the town, they decided to pop down the road, buy a nice bottle of wine and share it back in their room. They asked for the bill but due to the busyness of the staff had to wait fifteen minutes to pay. Unbeknownst to them as their irritation grew, the delay would save at least one of their lives.

Now paid up and on their way, Adam decided he'd dump the camera back in the room before they set off for their wine. Jenny would wait in reception. Before they had a chance to move, though, they heard what sounded like a thunderclap. Must be someone slamming a shutter, said Adam. That was no shutter, said Jenny. And, right before their eyes, one side of the hotel slumped forward and crashed down in a billow of dust, landing in a mighty heap of rubble. Small segments of roofing balanced precariously on the few remaining supports, stairwells stuck out like cracked ribs on a brutalised skeleton, white metal balcony guards were piled like pick-up-sticks on the shattered concrete. They couldn't believe it. Their beautiful hotel reduced to this.

People were screaming and running, it was chaos. Eventually everyone was directed to the games room where a register was taken. It was horrible. There were so many not present to answer when their names were called. Everyone assumed the worst – they must be lying beneath the remains of the fallen rooms. There could be very little hope. The woman reading out the names broke down, sobbing, and someone else had to take over.

Amazingly, there was no one in the rooms when that side of the hotel disintegrated. Everyone was moved to another hotel. The next morning they returned to view the wreckage in the revealing light of day. There was the ceiling of their room, now hanging against the door of the room across the corridor. There on the rubble was Adam's beach towel. Beside it lay an exploded TV and, infinitely more disturbing, a mattress covered by a massive slab of concrete. But for the grace of God, there went they.

Adam and Jenny abandoned their holiday and flew home as soon as they could. Yet though they left the hotel, the hotel would not leave them. The what-ifs and if-onlys came to haunt them. What if it had happened but two minutes later? Adam would surely have been killed. What if the waiter had been quicker to bring the bill? What if the collapse had occurred later that night? All thirty guests would have been crushed and mangled.

The Ministry of Tourism on Mallorca carried out an investigation and concluded that the hotel had collapsed due to defective building materials. Thomson would offer a full refund to all guests, as well as free counselling. But Adam and Jenny demanded further compensation for the trauma they had endured and were still enduring.

Various conclusions can be drawn from this. First – mock not the dragon, lest his fiery breath consume your hopes. Second – be not proud. Even posh hotels can do a swan dive. And third – great holidays can create memories that stick for a lifetime. So can Holidays from Hell. So, next time you book your break away, think on. You could end up in therapy, or in a body bag. Here's hoping you wind up in clover.

4 Through the booking glass – adventures in blunderland

Already in this tome we've seen accidents, illnesses, angry animals, rampaging fungi, violent nutters and dangers of many kinds. But at least the holidays themselves were properly organised. The following stories reveal what can happen when trips are set up *without* due care and attention, when lines of communication break down, when things go pear-shaped in general. These are the most common Holidays from Hell, where the getting-there most certainly wasn't half the fun. Read on, and weep.

The ones with all the waiting

Holidays from Hell manifest themselves in many diabolical ways. And, as most holidays in these technologically advanced times begin at the airport, that's often when the stench of sulphur first invades the nostrils of the wretched travellers. In the last decade, flight delays have got worse and worse, to the extent that fewer than one in three holiday flights leave on time. The Walker and Parks families, along with Alexandra Smithson, were just a few of the sufferers. They should have been flying from Manchester to Ibiza at 11 at night. But, predictably, it was not to be.

At the airport, Britannia Airways announced that their flight was delayed and that, around midnight, coaches would arrive to whisk the unlucky passengers to more-than-reasonable hotel accommodation. Fair enough, they all thought, no vacation passes without its problems, best to get them over with before the holiday has really begun. Such an attitude was to be expected from the British. Lords of endurance, we hold as heroes the likes of Captain Scott, Ernest Shackleton and Ellen MacArthur, people who laugh in the face of disaster and defy the risk of lonely death. We take great pride in dealing with whatever comes our way.

But come two in the morning, no call had come to guide the waiting passengers to their coaches. Three o'clock passed, then four. Eight hours were whiled away in the open-plan discomfort of the seating areas. At last, come seven, the news shot through the patient crowd like a gust of pure happiness. We're away! Into the departure lounge they scurried, suddenly bright-eyed and bushy-tailed. They snapped up their duty frees with glad and greedy fingers and ... ten minutes later they were told to put it all back on the shelves and go back outside again.

Now, we Brits are patient. The fact that no one has seriously attempted to blow up Parliament since 1605 is testament to that. But this latest blow, a further unexplained addition to the hours of listless tedium they'd already suffered, sent the passengers into uproar. Fists were clenched and ready to fly. The Thomson reps were in mortal danger. How they must have given thanks for the Lord's bounty when they discovered that the coaches had finally arrived.

Calming somewhat now that they could see at least *something* was being done to ease their plight, the passengers allowed themselves to be carted off to a hotel, where they stayed for a further nine hours. But they didn't stay calm when, having been driven back to the airport, they were sent to a departure gate that they would quite clearly not be departing from. One passenger seized the staff microphone and demanded that a Britannia rep make their way to Gate 204 where a planeful of passengers were getting ... really ... cheesed ... off.

Eventually a rep did appear to face this most unmusical music. For her it was a nightmare. The plane, she said, had a technical fault and was, er, somewhere in the airport, getting fixed, and would be ready to leave, er, when it was fixed. Plainly, this was not the explanation the irate travellers wanted to hear and, before long, the rep was led away in floods of guilty tears.

But all bad things come to an end. After twenty-three long, long hours the flight from Manchester to Ibiza did take off. The ordeal was surely now over. Let the celebrations commence!

Sadly, this was no ordinary ordeal. It was the *real* ordeal. After twenty minutes in the sky, the relieved passengers were shaken from their complacent belief that nothing else could go wrong when the plane began to shudder dramatically. Those sitting beside the right engine saw flames shooting across the wing. Alexandra Smithson, for one, was convinced they were about to spiral down into oblivion.

On comes the pilot. Don't worry, we're simply suffering a recurrence of the original technical fault (how bad *was* this fault, that they couldn't fix it in 23 hours?). So the plane made a forced landing at Gatwick, still, you will note, some considerable distance from the Balearic Islands. No fewer than seventy passengers had had enough and refused to continue their journey. Those that did arrived in Ibiza some twenty-seven hours late.

Yet, for the Walkers, it was *still* not over. When a rep tried to put them on the wrong coach, they protested, only to hear him say 'Look, it's six in the morning, there's nothing I can do. Just get on the coach and we'll sort it all out when you've had some sleep'. So they did. And when they got to the hotel they discovered, as they had suspected, that there were no reservations in their name. After eight hours sat at the airport, nine at the hotel, a near-riot at the departure gate, and a flight in a burning plane, twenty-seven hours trying to keep the kids from freaking out, they'd been sent to the wrong hotel. For their pains, Thomson offered them £200 compensation. Britannia, meanwhile, claimed that their first flight had merely suffered an engine surge – the flames, in fact, signalled no danger to anyone. Recompense was set at £45 each.

The ones where worlds collide

Young lovers Martin Fletcher and Stella Wright understood how love must be cherished and protected, for it gives back so much more than it takes. This was why they decided on a trip to Palma, Mallorca. It was a chance to be young and together, to enjoy the sun, the sand and the sangria, to revel in the full blooming of love while other young couples similarly cavorted around them. Surely the tour operator First Choice recognised it also – why not leave the hotel booking to them?

This, as it turned out, was a grave error. But it didn't seem so initially. When they booked into the Hotel Fabiola they were taken by its smart décor, cleanliness and efficiency. They were a little surprised when the receptionist informed them that there were alarms on the walls of their room that they musn't push, but not overly so. It was next morning before they realised the scale of their plight. Arriving down for breakfast, they noted a collection of zimmer frames, walking sticks and wheelchairs at the bottom of the stairs, as if prepared for a regiment returning from a particularly bloody war. It was odd, very odd. Then, walking into the dining-room, they had their explanation. The place was packed with oldies, very old oldies, many of them being spoon-fed by white-clad assistants. Martin and Stella saw to their horror that they were the Fabiola's youngest guests by a good half a century.

Surely there must be some mistake? Sadly, no. Inquiries revealed that the three-star Hotel Fabiola was better known as the Residencia Fabiola: A Mediterranean Residence for your Retirement, though First Choice would occasionally use it for their younger clients. On learning this, fun-seeking Martin and Stella asked to be moved to a more appropriate setting, feeling they didn't have much in common with people who'd served with distinction in the Zulu War. But nothing doing, Mallorca was full up.

And so they had to stay, with proceedings becoming ever more bizarre. Sunbathing by the pool, they were surrounded by oldies waving thin rubber sticks in small circles, and performing other creepy aerobics. At dinner once, an ancient gentleman opposite their table lost control of his bowels. He was quickly helped away, but he'd left a clear watermark that was no aid to their digestion. Going out on the town, they enjoyed a few drinks in the banging clubs then, having been informed by the cab-drivers that it was highly unusual to take young people back to the Fabiola, they had to creep in silence down the corridors for fear of disturbing the wrinkly guests. Worst of all was the morning when, coming down to the lobby, they saw a coffin being carried through reception. A blessing was performed in the hotel chapel, then the coffin was brought back to a hearse waiting outside. Somehow it seemed to make a mockery of Boney M's famous celebration, 'Hooray! Hooray! It's a holi-holiday!'

It wasn't that Martin and Stella disliked old people. In fact, they planned to be old themselves one day. But they had wanted a vacation that centred around peach schnapps and passion, rather than corns and colostomy bags. On their return, having spent £748 on a bad time, they demanded compensation. First Choice insisted the Fabiola was a three-star hotel, but still offered £450.

And herein lies the moral to the tale. He who leaves the hotel booking to the tour operator shall be bothered by the smell of wee for evermore. Expert Frank Barrett put it another way. Leaving it to the operator is like going on a blind date. You could end up with Denise Van Outen, he said, or it could be Ann Widdecombe. And the odds are heavily stacked on Widdecombe.

This was the case for poor Zoe Baggaley and Gillian Knight. Both were 64, but still good-time girls at heart, who liked nothing better than a good knees-up and sing-along in the local. They were born to hokey cokey, if you get the drift. Yet they were 64 and, when they booked a holiday in Ibiza, again through First Choice, they weren't looking for anything other than a nice, quiet hotel where they could spend maybe an hour on the beach in the morning, and an hour on the balcony in the afternoon. You know – somewhere *nice*. Problem was, they too left the hotel booking to First Choice, and First Choice did not choose one from the brochure perused by Zoe and Gillian. Instead, they picked one from their specialist 2wentys brochure, and booked the ladies in on the notoriously raucous San Antonio Bay, at a hotel marked in the brochure as 'blockrockin' – a sure bet when it comes down to full-on 2wentys action!'

The hotel itself was fine. But, as you'd expect, the place was packed to the rafters with leering, beering lads and lasses, running through the corridors, slamming doors, mooning for England and ensuring the banging techno was permanently set at 11. Zoe and Gillian tried to grin and bear it but, after several sleepless nights when their angry thumps on the walls and ceiling were treated only as interesting percussive breaks, they gave up. They couldn't even grab a couple of hours' kip in the afternoon – even then the tumult was deafening.

After four nights, enough was enough. At three in the morning, they packed up their gear and demanded a change of hotel. The rep said it was impossible. They replied that they were packed and leaving, so the rep relented, took an extra £40 from each of them and gave them a scrap of paper bearing the name of their new apartment. And how would they get there? Well, said the rep in an annoyingly haughty manner, you get in a taxi and go. So they did. As Zoe put it as 'Peace and Desire' had boomed out at incredible volume each night, 'Never mind the desire, give me some peace'.

Zoe and Gillian paid £258 for their unwanted techno masterclass. First Choice claimed that they had not specifically requested a quiet hotel when they booked. Nevertheless, the ladies were refunded to the tune of £134. Rest assured they did not use it to purchase the latest by Ivan van Dahl.

It's not only the obvious resorts that bring problems like those faced by Zoe and Gillian. You'd think, for instance, that Cyprus would be safe. When the Bailey family booked a last-minute holiday at Ayia Napa, on the coast just south of Famagusta, they were after peace and quiet. Dad, after all, was a policeman by trade and aching to get away from any form of disturbance. They told their booking agent their requirements, and these were presumably passed on to First Choice. However, the hotel allocated to them on their arrival, as with Zoe and Gillian, was chosen from that now-infamous 2wentys brochure. That's right – it was blockrockin' time for the Baileys.

Now, the minimum age for guests at the hotel was seventeen. The Baileys' two kids were seven and eight and totally unsuited to the dusk-till-dawn partying around them. The first night was a disaster. Just as the family were going to bed, everyone else was just starting to kick out the jams. The balconies around them were soon filled with drunken youngsters cackling and bellowing. There was plenty of nudity, with one naked fellow openly urinating on the patio doors below them. It really wasn't for kids.

The next day the Baileys asked to be moved to a different hotel. They were told they could upgrade to a three-star establishment, also in Ayia Napa, but that it would cost them £1500. This, in effect, would mean writing off their present holiday – not something they could afford to do. Alternatively, they could be moved to another section of their present hotel. But that would place them beside the legendarily pumping River Reggae Club, open from twelve till seven in the morning. They'd just have to grimace and bear it.

And so they did. Every night they'd try to shut out the raucous roar of the wild festivities. Every day their poolside relaxation was wrecked by hungover hoolies and their boisterous cavorting. They had taken over the complex. There was no escape. The Baileys had paid £624 for their two-week holiday. They later accepted £550 in compensation.

Two important points arise from this story. The first was made by First Choice who admitted that when people book holidays where accommodation is allocated on arrival, there is no guarantee where it will be and what it will be like. They strongly advised people to book from the brochure. The second point would be made by anyone within the travel industry. When you buy a cheap holiday, you don't want it to be cheap *and* nasty. Unfortunately, because it's cheap it's almost *bound* to be nasty. You always get what you pay for. Always.

The one with the disappearing holiday

Some holidays are hellish in their failure to ever take place. There you are, toiling away like a workaholic, obsessive-compulsive bee, trying to get everything done and in order before departure and then, BANG, all your plans are wrecked by a single phone-call from the travel agent. Sorry, your holiday's off. It's the end already. *Fin*, as the French would have it. You've got nothing to do for two weeks but loaf around the house, eating junk food and wishing you could punch Kilroy's lights out. *Carpe diem* loses its meaning when your hotly anticipated vacation has been terminated forthwith.

Just such trouble arrived at the door of Maggie Smith. Suffering from severe arthritis, she had got into the wise habit of booking her holidays extremely early and ensuring that the accommodation would be suitable for one with such a debilitating problem. This year, via Cosmos, she was booked into the Hotel Conquistador on Tenerife. She'd been before, had a wonderful time, and was pleased to be returning.

Then, just as she'd zipped the final zip on her suitcase, BANG, it's Cosmos. Awfully sorry, but your holiday's a no-no. Hotel's overbooked. Can't be helped. Sorry. But, says Maggie, I booked this eleven months ago – this is a disgrace! Sorry, it's the hotel's fault, not ours. Well then, says Maggie, I want my money back right now. Ah, replies the agent, that will take approximately six weeks. Like Hell it will, says Maggie (who's something of a feisty lady), I'll be down there at 9.30 tomorrow morning and you'd better have my money waiting for me.

Now began the usual messing around. Companies are keen to give discounts for early bookings, but most reluctant to give compensation for cancellations. If you cancel your holiday, you'll probably lose your money. If they cancel it, you'll be hard pressed to get your money back quickly. It's a kind of lose-lose situation.

As far as Maggie was concerned, she and her husband Don had paid £1424 for their aborted trip to Tenerife. Cosmos offered her £15 for her thwarted dreams. Being a feisty lady, she told them where to stick their £15 and held out for £400. Her persistence is a lesson to us all. As Michael Jackson so pertinently put it back in 1979, don't stop (till you get enough).

The one with the funny-looking airport

So, we've seen that getting there is not necessarily half the fun. Indeed, it can be all the horror. But what about those sad cases where your travelling is efficient, enjoyable but in totally the wrong direction? What happens when they take you to the wrong place?

Such a tale is that of Alfie Peters and Cyril Hussey, longtime friends and both veterans of the Second World War, when they booked themselves a Thomson holiday on Crete. For Alfie and Cyril this had become an annual event. Where possible, they'd always stay in the same quiet, relaxing hotel, spending their days in a local taverna, benignly watching the world go by with, as they put it, 'a little drop of medicine to keep us going'. They'd made friends on the island and, as former British soldiers, found the natives to be especially welcoming.

This particular year, though, their trip was to be tinged with sadness. Now both getting on a bit and finding walking difficult even with the aid of a cane, they'd decided that this would be their last visit. It would serve as a sweet farewell to their friends, to Crete and to holidays in general. The memories would come flooding back, and maybe a few more good ones would be created.

It all began at Gatwick, when the pair went to the Thomson desk to wait for a buggy that would deliver them to the departure gate. They were met by a rep who asked them to sit down and make themselves comfortable – they would be seen to shortly. But they weren't seen to shortly. Indeed they waited some considerable time. Eventually, when a buggy did trundle into view, the rep called out for the driver to hold on, she had two late passengers for him. 'But we weren't late,' explained the old fellows later, 'We'd been sitting there for an hour.'

Nevertheless, despite the inconvenience, they were on their way. Soon they'd be sipping ouzos with their old buddies in the taverna. The buggy dropped them at the aircraft, they struggled to their seats and, before long, the plane had made its final approach and landed.

Unfortunately, it hadn't landed on Crete. Alfie thought the airport looked strange as he and Cyril were being wheeled through it, and he asked the rep about it. It turned out they'd come to Kefallinia. Now, this wasn't necessarily a disaster. Kefallinia, just south of Corfu, is one of the Ionian Islands off the west coast of Greece, while Crete is situated to the country's south-east, only 271 miles away. Something could surely be done.

Thomson claim that they offered to reimburse Alfie and

Cyril or, if they wished, to fly them back to London and then on to Crete, where they'd arrive that same day. Alfie and Cyril tell an entirely different story. They say their aeroplane had already departed and couldn't possibly have taken them back to England. And when they suggested that they might be taken to their proper destination by boat they were told that they'd have to island-hop, which would use up most of their fortnight.

So, deciding to cut their losses, they stayed on Kefallinia, an island later described by Alfie as 'a lump of rock put in the middle of nowhere'. That seems a little unfair. After all, Kefallinia is a popular resort of startling craggy rocks and quiet bays. It produces wonderful oils and excellent wines and it boasts a proud history – its inhabitants having gone with Odysseus to the Trojan War. But it wasn't what Alfie and Cyril had paid for, a place they knew was suited to their wants and special needs.

Hoping for a five-star hotel 'with everything laid on', they were booked into a hotel from the outside resembling a multi-storey car park. Inside, it was well-appointed but open-plan and multi-levelled, far from the cosy taverna they'd set their hearts on. It wasn't ideally located either. There was a lift to the beach, but there the soft sand made it impossible for the veterans to walk. Out the back of the hotel, the road up to the main drag was so steep they couldn't possibly negotiate it.

So there they were, these poor old geezers, pretty much

confined to their hotel and feeling not unlike prisoners of war. Their holiday ruined, they just had to grin and bear it till it was time to go home. Eight months later, describing their Holiday from Hell, they were resigned to the fact that they would never say goodbye to Crete. Thomson said they sincerely regretted the misunderstanding, but there was no record of Alfie and Cyril complaining during their stay. Still, the company did return £700 of the £1358 the old men had paid.

The message here, it seems, is Beware the Buggy. It may feel like a slog when you're dragging your suitcases and children through security checks and duty free areas, then along badly carpeted walkways to a departure gate seemingly situated in another county, but at least you're in control. On the dreaded buggy, you have no real idea where you're going. You're facing the wrong way for a start. All you can be sure of is that the person driving is less concerned with getting you to the right plane than with whether they'll have ketchup or HP sauce on their lunchtime fish fingers.

Let's face it, British holidaymakers, almost without exception, would board any plane they were buggied to, convinced that all was right and correct. There's good reason for it, too. Historically speaking, we are born of peasants who for hundreds of years believed that their lords and masters would treat them fairly. The argument follows then that anyone driving a buggy – a buggy being a righteous status symbol at any airport – is bound to be careful, wise and decent. Do we ever consider that the buggy's driver might be a narky jobsworth who doesn't care if he sends you to Kefallinia by mistake because a) you can't get him into trouble as you've only ever seen the back of his head and b) you can't do anything about it anyway – you're in Kefallinia? No, we most certainly do not.

So watch out for buggy drivers. You don't know them. You don't know what they're thinking. And they may just wish you harm.

5 Clouds without silver linings

Most holidaymakers base their choice of destination on the weather. Whether they're skiing, boating, walking or simply slobbing out on the beach, they like the temperature and wind-speed to be suitable. Maybe this annoys the Weather Gods. Maybe they believe we should accept the weather we're given, like good little mortals. Their anger at our defiance would explain why so many thousands of holidays are wrecked by the elements. The following stories feature just a small sample of the meteorological mayhem that takes place each year.

The one with all the wind

If there's one vital lesson prospective travellers need to learn it's Don't Believe The Brochure. Many people believe that the glossy books, magazines and pamphlets handed out by travel companies and agents contain official Consumers Association reports on resorts. They most assuredly do not. They contain advertisements for resorts, knocked up by people who desperately want you to go there. Resorts are shown at their very best, when the bright sun brings a pleasing gleam to both buildings and vegetation. The water and the sky are always of the most gratifying blue. These adverts never fail to present resorts as paradisaical oases of beauty and luxury and there is never, ever a suggestion that this situation might rapidly change.

So it was with an Airtours trip to the Dominican Republic. What a heaven on Earth it appeared to be. Lolling in the Caribbean to the immediate west are Cuba and Jamaica. To the east Puerto Rico and the lazily curving chain of the Leeward and Windward Islands, featuring the exotic charms of Antigua, Martinique and Barbados. Beyond this, the Dominican Republic shares its island with the mysterious voodoo nation of Haiti. Could it be more attractively situated? Could the sand be any whiter, the sea any bluer, the palm trees any more beautiful? And all for £400. *Result*! It was a trip that May Churchill, Matt West and his partner Sue simply could not miss.

But, as said above, brochures never tell the whole truth. And one thing this brochure failed to stress was that the British holiday season heavily overlaps the Caribbean hurricane season, stretching from June to October. This was something May Churchill began to contemplate with much trepidation when, watching TV in her hotel room, she heard reports that a hurricane was heading their way. It didn't sound like much fun, in fact it sounded like her worst nightmare, so she went to the Airtours rep and asked to be flown home straight away. Damn the cost, she just wanted out before the big wind hit. It took a while for the rep to calm her. Really, there was no call for alarm. Reluctantly, May returned to her room.

The next morning, Matt and Sue felt a creeping sense of horror as TV reports showed the devastation on Puerto Rico as Hurricane Georges swept across it. And now it was heading west, straight towards the Dominican Republic. Matt and Sue went to their Thomson's rep, asking if they could be moved. Like May, they were told that there was nothing to fear.

But there was. There was an awful lot to fear. Later that day May, Matt and the other guests, all of them glued to their tellies and keeping a watchful eye on the hurricane's progress, were hugely disturbed when their sets went dead. The reps were now the only source of information and when Matt's told him that from that moment she was no longer responsible for their safety and well-being, all authority being transferred to the hotel, he knew there was major trouble ahead.

May Churchill was similarly perturbed when she found herself being handed two candles, a bottle of water and a sandwich – apparently this passes for a hurricane survival kit around those parts. She was also told to barricade her windows with a mattress and to stay in the bathroom where she and her friends would be safe. Matt, meanwhile, had been advised to pack his bags and stack them on top of the wardrobe, to take all mirrors and pictures off the walls and place the TV set on the floor. Then he should take his place in the casino by no later than 11 o'clock. Recognising the wisdom of removing all mirrors in his room, to minimise the risk of shattered glass flying everywhere, he was more than uncomfortable to discover that the hotel's safe haven, the casino, was surrounded on all sides by mirrors.

When the hurricane hit, May was huddled in the bathroom with her friends. She could not believe the violence of the storm but nevertheless felt reasonably secure. Then the room's window came through and the vandal wind began its orgy of destruction within. Still it was bearable in the bathroom. Bearable, that is, until the roaring tempest began to wrench off the ceiling. In a panic, they opened the door and ran out onto the landing. There was nowhere to go. All May remembers is the screaming, both hers and everyone else's. Everyone screaming for their very lives.

Suddenly, there was a deathly stillness. It seemed the hurricane's monstrous appetite for destruction had been sated. May recalls the strangeness of the complete silence, then the burst of cheering and laughter as the guests rushed out onto their balconies, keen to see the sun and celebrate their survival. And then she recalls the loud and strident shouts of the hotel manager as he ordered everyone to get back inside. It was not over. They were merely enjoying a brief respite in the hurricane's eye.

And just as abruptly as the silence had fallen, the storm renewed its assault. Only this time it was twice as bad. Now unprotected, May ran through the corridors, shrieking in terror, battering on doors, begging to be let in to a place of safety. But no one could hear her desperate pleas in the turmoil. On she ran, doors flying past her, ceilings crashing down around her, until a man grabbed her and dragged her under some stairs. And here she sat, convinced the windy reaper was about to claim her, for a further three hours. At the passing of the hurricane, she remembers the first chirpings of the birds as the most beautiful sound she's ever heard.

The damage caused by Hurricane Georges was immense. Trees had been pulled out by their roots, such was its appalling force. Naturally, the guests felt they really ought to be compensated for their night of terror, and for the storm's haphazard rearrangement of the resort, which no longer resembled the paradise pictured in the brochures. May was particularly annoyed at her rep's attitude when she said May should just be glad she was still alive, adding that she, the rep, had been through it too.

After all, unlike the rep, May had paid £850 and Matt and Sue £1138. But it was not to be. Under the regulations, tour operators are not required to move their customers, or even to offer that choice. Thomson apologised to Matt, but added that their brochure did mention the possibility of bad weather. Airtours, meantime, told May they had no record of her request to be moved and said that they had done their best according to the local civil defence authority.

So, no windfall for May or Matt (ho ho ho).

The one with all the heaving

A life on the ocean wave – what excitement it promises, what adventure, what romance. Countless generations have dreamt of a buccaneering existence, bobbing defiantly above the vasty deep, daring to breathe the strangely scented air of mysterious shores, drinking strong rum and singing shanties to the spouting whales. Of course, the reality was often quite different.

These days the closest most of us ever get to a piratical life (aside from the odd case of scurvy in Glasgow) is on a holiday cruise. And not too many of us go on those. After all, a cruise has traditionally been viewed as the Rolls Royce of holidays and, though it's not as heartbreakingly expensive as it used to be, it's still pretty pricey.

Barry recognised this when he booked himself and his

wife Karen onto the good ship *Topaz* for the Thomson European Wonders Cruise. But he wanted to give his beloved a surprise present for their 23rd anniversary and, as they'd never been abroad before, he spared no expense. Also on board would be Emma and Peter, a younger couple who thought the trip – taking in Marseilles, Barcelona and several spots in Italy – would give them the highlights of many of the places they'd really like to visit.

Having boarded the ship at Palma on Mallorca, Barry and Karen just could not believe their luck. The cabins were well-appointed and, without exception, the crew referred to them as Madame and Monsieur. This was the life. Having settled in, they were invited down to the banqueting hall, where all the tables were covered with high-quality linens and set with gleaming cutlery. All the passengers wore smart evening dress, and a cabaret show began, a real extravaganza with a troupe of young singers and dancers rocking and rolling their way through an exuberant *Grease*-style revue. Meanwhile the ship weighed anchor and they were off to Italy. Karen was in a state of wonder. With no previous experience on the water at all, she was convinced she'd be seasick, yet they'd left port without her even noticing. She was going to be fine. She said later that she and Barry kept pinching each other to prove it was all real.

Unfortunately, the happy impression that they were gliding across a mill pond did not last for long. Within the hour, the ship hit choppy waters and it was officially suggested that the passengers take their seasickness tablets. When this is *officially* suggested you can bet your bottom dollar there's going to be some champion hurling, and there was – sick bags everywhere. Karen held on for a while but, when she went up on deck and first saw the big swells of the white-capped waves, she fell instantly against the railings and loudly emptied her belly into the Mediterranean.

With the winds rising to gale force, the *Topaz* made its queasy way across the sea and safely reached Italy. They were a day late but the passengers were too relieved to be on dry land to worry about minor details like that. Descending onto the waterfront, Karen said she'd been so frightened and sick she felt like doing a John Paul II and snogging the tarmac.

The two days they spent in Italy certainly helped the memory of their bad passage to fade considerably. They marvelled at the Vatican, the Coliseum, the leaning tower of Pisa, thrilling to the exceptional paintings, sculptures and architecture that surrounded them. Returning to the *Topaz* at Livorno, they hoped that the cultured calm of the last 48 hours would continue onboard.

But it was not to be. Within the hour, yet again they sailed into poor weather, and this time it was horrendous. They were scheduled to be heading for Marseilles but, the captain informed them, they were re-routing straight to Barcelona in order to miss the worst of the storm.

Nevertheless, it was still bad. You could hear the contents of the ship being tossed from one side to the other as the boat lurched on the increasingly angry waves. People were skidding across the floors, others were gripping their seats for dear life. Karen remembers the terrible creaking of the vessel as it struggled along. No one could keep thoughts of the *Titanic* from their mind for long. At one point, Karen noticed one man with his eyes 'out on stalks'. She followed his gaze and discovered he was staring in horror at a massive wall of water to their starboard. 'Don't look,' she advised him. 'Just don't look.' But, inside, she was convinced that this was it, this was where the boat would tip over and all hands would be lost.

Yet with fortune and the captain's skill on their side, they sailed through the night and made it to Barcelona. At last, thought Peter, we can escape this churning nightmare and go home. By planc. He was not the only one greedy for a chance to abandon ship. But all hopes of early deliverance were dashed when the captain announced that the port of Barcelona had been closed due to the stinking weather. He had no choice but to turn the vessel around and head straight for their final destination, back to Palma. The Spanish mainland and liberty from fear would remain a faint shadow on the horizon.

None of the passengers could believe this dreadful turn of events. After all they'd been through, here they were being taken back out into what they construed to be mortal danger. This was supposed to be a luxury cruise, damn it, not a teeth-rattling, stomach-churning endurance test. Ganging together, as people do in times of peril, they demanded a meeting with the captain and the Thomson reps.

Naturally, the atmosphere at the meeting was highly charged. The passengers were keen to find out why they'd ever left Palma when weather reports had stated that the area would be unsafe throughout the week. The captain tried to explain that, though the passengers were feeling some discomfort, the ship wasn't, hadn't been and wouldn't be in any real danger. No one was having that one. The affair became ever more heated until the captain told one particularly vociferous individual that if he thought he could sail the ship better he was welcome to go up onto the bridge and try. Go on, Pugwash, let's see how *you* do.

The conference resolved nothing, and the passengers were forced to knuckle down and see out the storm. Courageously, the entertainers tried to raise spirits with songs of joy and tales of laughter, but they just reminded people of the brave band who were still playing when the *Titanic* slipped into the icy deep. They knew Palma was still very far away.

Karen later described the experience as 'like being on a never-ending rollercoaster', and it was rough indeed. As the weather worsened, the corridors were dangerously slanted. At the high end, people were clinging to the door frames for dear life. Others slid down and bashed into the wall below. Every time the ship was turned to aim at Palma, waves would hit the side. Everyone thought capsize was imminent. Davy Jones' Locker, here we come.

After two days' continuous sailing across the unruly sea, they finally made it to Mallorca. The island, too, was suffering in the storm, with waves assaulting the rocky shoreline and palm trees bowing before the brutal force of the wind. The devastation brought home to everyone exactly what kind of storm they'd braved (or, in most cases, cowered beneath). Trees had been plucked from the ground and tossed aside. Concrete walls had been smashed. Boats lay broken and half submerged in the harbour. It had clearly been a bad one. What on Earth had they been doing in the middle of it?

Barry and Karen had paid £1564 for their anniversary cruise, and Emma and Peter had shelled out £1038. You'd have thought that, given their trip was light years from the heavenly experience promised by the brochure, they'd have been compensated to the tune of, ooh, £1564 and £1038. But look more closely at that cruise brochure. In the small print you will find that the tour operator is protected against force majeure – dictionary-defined as 'an unforeseeable and uncontrollable course of events, excusing one from fulfilling a contract'. Thomson reiterated the captain's line that the passage may have been uncomfortable but the ship was never in any danger.

Whether or not the storm that hit the *Topaz* could be regarded as 'unforeseeable' is certainly arguable. But forecast mistakes are made often. After all, it wasn't so long ago that Michael Fish and his fellow meteorological maestros swore blind that there would be no hurricane. And what happened then? We all woke the next day to find the car and the garden shed in the attic. Force majeure, indeed.

The ones with all the snow

Despite the settings of most of the Holidays from Hell included herein, not everyone wants a sun-soaked vacation. Every year, thousands flock to the mountains for an opportunity to strap two thin pieces of wood to their feet and fly headlong down dangerously steep slopes. Apparently, they love it, the mad fools.

Yet the weather that creates the picturesque mountain settings they so enjoy can also quickly turn destroyer. This is what Gary, Amy and Sarah discovered when they took a skiing holiday in the French Alps. They'd hoped for excellent conditions, heavy snowfalls having been reported. But unfortunately there had been too much snow, and it was still falling. It was announced that the slopes were now too hazardous and should be abandoned. On their return to their chalet, they looked like disconsolate shadows in the blizzard.

Once the snow had stopped, though, they decided at least to get some fresh air. They walked down the road to view the lake nearby. All was well, the air crisp and invigorating, the scenery quite spectacular. Then suddenly they heard a ferocious roar above them. They looked up to see vast, billowing clouds of snow rampaging down towards them. Avalanche! Running for their lives, they got about as far as you can in two seconds before being totally engulfed in the freezing torrent. Over and over they were spun, desperately struggling to stay upright, trying to swim to the surface as the white wave threatened to bury them alive.

Fortunately for the threesome, the lake took the full force of the avalanche and they were hit only by its dying edges. Interred in only shallow graves, they managed to dig themselves out without too much trouble. Looking out at the violently altered snowscape, they recognised their outrageous luck and literally jumped for joy at still being alive.

A few weeks later, luck was in shorter supply. Part-time fireman Simon Marks, his brother Alexander and their young families also took a break among the Alps. The brothers had been before, but for the children it was a thrilling first. On arrival conditions were perfect. The adults enjoyed their skiing while the kids rolled around on tiny snowboards and joyfully dug dens in the snow.

But the fun wasn't to last as the weather turned bad.

The resort was suffering its heaviest snowfall in 100 years. Worse still, fluctuating temperatures were destabilising the drifts higher up in the mountains, and vast fields of snow were on the move downwards. Everyone entertained themselves in their chalets and hotels. They had no choice, the roads were blocked, leaving 3500 holidaymakers cut off from the outside world. And still the snow fell, making the next chalet just a murky blob in the swirling gloom.

And then it came. About four in the afternoon, the families heard a deafening clamour as a massive avalanche swooped down upon them. The parents seized their children and held them to the floor, covering their bodies with their own, expecting the chalet to explode around them under the force of the onrushing snow. But it never happened. The white surge had only clipped them. Still, looking out the window was like peering into an operating washing machine. Clearly not everyone would have survived unscathed.

Simon and Alexander took flashlights and went out to investigate. It was by now dark and bitter cold, -10°C and falling. They walked over a new mound of snow from which protruded the back bumpers of buried cars. People were digging desperately. Keen to help, they were directed to a hotel where casualties were already being brought in. You couldn't see the carpet for the bodies on the floor. Simon stayed to administer First Aid, Alexander went out to dig. The fresh heaps were so massive it was like seeking a needle in a haystack. It was tough and depressing work, and deeply distressing when a German voice in the darkness shouted out 'Kinder!'

The next morning revealed the full horror of the situation. Buildings had been decimated, smeared across the slopes. Cars had been twisted and crushed. What had been a charming mountainside hamlet was now an ugly stretch of rubble. The authorities launched an impressive rescue operation, the tourists being evacuated in a fleet of helicopters. Flying to safety, they looked down on the destruction wrought and wondered at their good fortune.

In one respect it was good that the Marks were there. Less able men could not have provided the same assistance. But the brothers have paid a price for leaving their cabin that night. They can't forget it. And neither should we. Should we – God forbid – ever end up in a similar scenario, wouldn't it be great if we all knew at least the rudiments of First Aid? Of course it would. So let's get learning.

The one with the unexpected rivers

Egypt – the very mention of the place sends the imagination into overload. The endlessly contemplating Sphinx crouched on the sweeping sands. The magnificent Pyramids, raised on the blood and toil of ancient thousands. The fantastically attractive queen embracing poisonous snakes rather than dishonour. The immense libraries, containing all human knowledge, being put to the torch by ignorant usurpers. So steeped in amazing history, so thrilling to the mind and senses. You really ought to get there before the Americans invade.

Morgan and Sharon were, quite rightly, expecting something special when they booked an Egyptian jaunt through Hayes and Jarvis. They couldn't wait to explore the fabulous temples and labyrinthine bazaars. And, a couple of glorious days in, they were still hungry for more.

But matters were about to take an unusual turn for the worse. It began to rain – for this arid region a weird and unexpected event. And it kept raining. Soon people were paddling ankle-deep in the streets. As the downpour grew ever heavier, such that you couldn't see out of the windows, the water rose above the bumpers of the cars, then higher. Stranded drivers were abandoning their vehicles to float off where they pleased.

Morgan and Sharon's hotel was badly affected. For a start, there was a total power failure, the only light in their room being a single candle sputtering in the middle of the floor. Next, as the flood backed up the drains, the water from the taps was coming out an unpleasant brown. The smell was disgusting, and it didn't help that Morgan was suffering from dreadful diarrhoea. Unable to sleep due to cramps and continual emergencies, all he could do was lie on the bed and prepare for his next hunched-over sprint to the bathroom.

Naturally, they asked their rep if they might be moved to a different hotel. Preferably one with electricity. But they were told not to worry, the power would be restored the next day. When it wasn't they asked again. There'd been a bit of a hold-up, it'll be tomorrow. Tomorrow, tomorrow, tomorrow – for four days and nights it continued.

Finally, normal service was resumed, and they could begin to enjoy the arcane delights of this extraordinary country. Trouble was, Morgan's bowels were still in explosive disorder so, before taking a coach to any of the mind-boggling monuments, they had to ensure there'd be frequent toilet stops, and that the monuments themselves had a Portaloo within reasonable running distance. After all, they didn't want to repeat the experiences of Ozzy Osbourne at the Alamo. Imagine it. 'Death to the infidel who pooped on the tomb of the great Pharaoh Ramses! May his blaspheming bum-hole be burned and its ashes cast to the four winds!' *That*'s no holiday, is it?

Thankfully for Morgan, the amenities were excellent. Without having to scour the street markets for giant-sized Pampers, he did fulfil his dream of standing in the shadow of the Pyramids. But fortune smiled less warmly on him after his return home. Having spent £818 on their trip into the heart of exotica, only to spend days and nights in their dark and smelly room, he and Sharon were offered only £50 compensation each. It seemed so little for a man who had lost so much, and so often.

6 Oh, I don't like to be beside the seaside

When we book a holiday abroad there are so many variables, so many aspects that are absolutely out of our control. And one of the most problematic is water. Now, water's perfectly fine and dandy when there's just a bit of it. You know, like when you heat some of it up and sit in it. But when there's lots of it, well, trouble is never very far behind. The following stories gather together just a few of water's diabolical tricks.

The one without Leo DiCaprio and Kate Winslet

Daah-dum, daah-dum, daah-dum, daah-dum-dum-dum-dum-dum-dum … Even without its accompanying crotchets and quavers, you can easily recognise this tune. Indeed, it's so famous, so fraught with dreadful meaning, and so deeply embedded in the public consciousness, you could probably guess it from a single Daah-dum. Affirmative, captain, it's John Williams' classic piece from *Jaws*, employed whenever the director wanted to notch the fear-factor up by several million degrees. Interestingly, when Steven Spielberg first heard the music, he thought Williams was taking the rise. It was too simple, too to-the-point. It was the work of a child, not a master composer. He was not happy at all. Then he played it alongside his footage and realised that it was actually marked by genius. It would contribute heavily to making the movie a classic and a mega-hit, and to launching Spielberg into the directorial Major Leagues. And even today, almost thirty years later, the music wordlessly conveys its message to us all. You know what it says. It says For God's sake, don't go near the water!

It's a message we should take seriously. After all, even the most cursory glance at the human body informs us that we don't belong in the water. We have no gills, no fins, no powerful tail to drive and guide us. We don't have the lips to suck up plankton, the teeth to tear mouthfuls from larger prey. We can't even break into a lobster without the aid of a hammer. How pathetic would *that* look on the ocean floor? No, we must face it, we'd make rubbish fish. Not even Australia's super-Olympian, the mighty Thorpedo himself, would cut it among the denizens of the vasty deep.

And it's not just our own inadequacies that should

compel us to steer clear of the Big Blue. The sea is not good for us. The salt, the microbes and the algae make us sick, quite apart from the chemicals, oil and raw sewage we pump in there ourselves. Beyond this, the creatures within are far from sympathetic to our cause. The molluscs will slice your toes with the sharp edges of their shells. The jellyfish will sting you, the crabs will nip you, even the prawns will stab you with their vicious little horns. And then, of course, returning to our earlier theme, there are the big boys. Have you ever imagined being eaten by a shark? Have you stared into those black, black eyes? Have you pictured yourself caught up to the waist in that merciless maw, being shaken with insane force from side to side, as the predator sends you into an insensibility from which there will be no recovery? And what if it belched on you? (Do sharks belch, or was that just a horrible dream?) Can you imagine the smell of a Great White's burp? It's all just too disgusting to contemplate. And we haven't even *mentioned* being sucked to death by a giant squid …

Yet despite all these horrors, and all the others not considered above, holiday-makers cannot resist the pull of the sea. Take Dave and Penny Block, for instance. They booked a mini-cruise from Cyprus to the Holy Land with Paradise Cruises. From the start it looked dodgy, and the couple were most disappointed with their ship, the 58-year-old *MV Romantica*. And it wasn't simply to do with the rather disturbing cover of the boat's brochure, picturing a bearded captain hugging a young boy. No, conditions onboard were not what you'd want from an ocean-going liner. Well, unless you're one of those freaky few who'd really like to know what it felt like to be aboard the *Titanic*.

For a start, on first entering their lodgings, the Blocks noted with some disapproval that their 'luxury apartment' had no toilet yet, just some guy working on a hole in the floor. The shower was a lukewarm trickle, the decorations were poor, with peeling paint everywhere. The cabin smelt, it was damp, there was no air-conditioning and you couldn't hear the ship's tannoy – bad news should the Kraken wake. Elsewhere on the *Romantica*, whole areas were blocked off and in disarray. Smoke alarms were hanging down from the ceilings, lights too, and water was dripping down over bare wiring. Up on deck, they noticed that the safety rails did not stretch all the way round the boat, leaving dangerous gaps through which the unwary could plummet to a watery grave. Furthermore, should there, God forbid, be any serious accident, it would be hard to reach many of the lifeboats as the deck was packed with long planks and massive rolls of carpet – carpet that really ought to have been rolled out and tacked to the ship's floors.

The crew's behaviour was no less shabby. To the Blocks they seemed not to know anything. They were unhelpful, sometimes even abusive. At one point Dave was told that if he didn't stop complaining he'd be confined to his quarters. No doubt, in times gone by, they would have administered a few sharp lashes from the cat. Once safely back in Cyprus, the Blocks went back to Paradise Cruises to complain some more. They did not, they said, believe the *Romantica* had been in any condition to set sail at all.

But Paradise disagreed, and the *Romantica* quickly disembarked once more, this time with the carpets properly laid. Of the 485 passengers onboard 120 were British, including Rodney and Emily Stodder, Mick and Dot Russel, and Judy Benson and her boyfriend Steven. The cruise was uneventful, a smooth groove across the ocean blue. That is, until the early hours of October 4th. Around five in the morning, the passengers were awoken by a turmoil below decks. The lights wouldn't work and there was a frighteningly strong smell of burning. Oh, Lord, fire in the hold!

Further petrified by the captain's loud tannoy announcement of 'Abandon ship! Abandon ship!', they pulled on their life-jackets and legged it up onto the deck. Within a couple of minutes, Rodney Stodder turned to see that the ship's funnel was now awash with flames. That's it, he thought, we're all fish-food. As the red distress flares screamed up into the night sky, then fell despondently into oblivion, everyone prayed there was someone, *anyone* out there to see them.

Once more, the crew were not much help. Dot Russel recalls them being more scared than the passengers.

Under the circumstances, you'd expect a degree of panic. On a sinking ship these days, people are unlikely to stand placidly to one side, nonchalantly playing a violin. But the panic here was accentuated by the crew's organisational deficiencies. Sitting in a lifeboat being lowered, Dot Russel was terrified when one end stuck, nearly tipping the passengers into the sea. Then, when they reached the water, the motor wouldn't start, one frustrated crew member hurling the motor-cover overboard in anger. He shouted in broken English for the passengers to find some oars, and that, according to Rodney Stodder, was when the passengers took over, organising themselves and rowing their way to safety, away from the burning vessel.

Back on board, Judy Benson was going from one lifeboat station to another. The panic now was getting bad. There were too many people at each station. There was shouting and pushing, men openly fighting each other. People were jumping from the deck into the water and trying to clamber into the lifeboats already launched, bringing a new danger of capsizing. Looking back from the lifeboats to the *Romantica*, it seemed impossible that all the people still on board could possibly fit into the single lifeboat remaining.

Fortunately, it didn't matter as another cruise ship had spotted the distress signals and had now arrived at the scene. The sun had his hero's hat on, too, for dawn broke just in time to aid the rescue operation. Everyone survived. But it could have been so different. If dawn hadn't broken, if the sea had been choppy, if the flares had gone unseen, it could have been a disaster. Nonsense, said the *Romantica*'s owners, and a year later compensation had still not been paid to the passengers.

The one with the murderous current

Aside from the toothy, spiky, poisonous creatures that live in it, the sea itself can be a mortally dangerous proposition. And not simply when gale-force winds whip it into a foamy frenzy. Where this writer lives, on the Somerset shore, the currents can be seen to fly sideways, parallel to the beach and on down to the mouths of the Brue and Parret rivers to the south. If you're foolish enough to enter the water when the red flags are flying, that's where you're going too. Even when the tide is out the beach can claim its victims. Only last year a little girl was killed when her father took her too far out onto the mud-flats. Many tourists have driven down to the water's edge, only to gape in surprise and horror as the incoming tide sweeps round behind them through the shallow gulleys, forcing them to flee towards the dunes on foot, abandoning their prized vehicles to be destroyed by the salty waves. We all know the sea can be powerful and merciless. But it also has tricks to catch out the unwary – deadly tricks.

This was not on the minds of Duncan and Catherine Parker when they took their son and daughter to Sfakaki on the Greek island of Crete. Booking through Manos Holidays, their brochure spoke of lovely, quiet beaches, perfect for families, and hopefully perfect for their family, too, this being their first trip away in three years. On arrival, it certainly looked perfect, so beautiful that they spent their first afternoon on their balcony in the Pavlos apartments, just looking and thinking how fortunate they were to have fallen so firmly on their feet.

Also staying in the apartments, though not together, were Maria Cable and George Moore. They'd arrived a few days before the Parker family. On her first day, with the temperature soaring into the eighties, Maria had quickly found the temptation of the water too much to resist and, skipping gingerly across the sand burning underfoot, she ran into the sea. She did not go far out, in fact she only went in up to her waist. But even then she felt the force of the current whipping around her legs and drawing her remorselessly away from the beach. She struggled with some difficulty back to the shore and, shocked by the danger that had suddenly come upon her, decided there and then to not go back into the water. When she mentioned the event to her apartment manager, he agreed that she should be careful. The water was not safe.

George Moore, meanwhile, had made the same discovery on his own. An RAF technician, he was a very strong swimmer, yet still he had trouble coming to grips with the Sfakaki currents. On his first day, he'd swum out some thirty metres then noticed that, within a mere ten minutes, he'd been carried some thirty metres along the shoreline. He asked some locals what they knew of the matter and they replied, yes, the current was notoriously powerful. Soon after this, back on the beach, George noticed two women in the water, clearly in distress. For some time they'd been trying to regain the sand, yet had been swept over a hundred metres out of their way. Plunging into the sea, he pulled them both to safety.

The Parker family were not aware of any of this as they sat congratulating themselves on their balcony. The next day, they spent the morning exploring the town then, as the heat rose, decided to visit the beach. It looked wonderful. People were relaxing by the bar at the beach's entrance, they were lolling on the sand, paddling in the warm water, revelling in their brief freedom from care. Duncan, Catherine and their daughter Sarah went directly into the water for a cooling dip and, after a few minutes, Catherine returned to their towels to sit with her son and read. But, just as she picked up her book and began to focus, she became conscious that all was not right. Call it a mother's intuition. She went back down to the sea's lapping edge and, scanning the glittering brine, realised that Sarah was having problems. Even more frightening, Duncan was further out, shouting at his daughter to get out of the water.

It must have been so hard to comprehend. Sarah, evidently distressed and rapidly tiring, struggling to reach the beach just a few yards away. Catherine called out to her, urging her to kick harder, before two men rushed in and pulled the girl out. And it was when Sarah was returned unharmed to her side that Catherine noticed that her husband was no longer anywhere to be seen. Frantically, she began to scan the waves, panic rising inside her. Behind her, George Moore and a friend saw the commotion and raced into the sea. But rapidly they, too, found themselves in trouble.

George felt his limbs tiring and hope receding when, rising to the crest of a wave, he saw Duncan some fifty yards away. He swam to him and gave him immediate mouth-to-mouth, desperately trying to force some air into his body. Then he started in to shore, pulling Duncan with him. Catherine watched all this with a trepidation that can only be imagined. She recalls her daughter turning to her and saying, 'It's all right, mum, dad's waved'.

But dad hadn't waved, his arm had simply flopped forward as George battled for both their lives. When the pair were about fifty yards out, the by-now exhausted George beckoned for help and more men splashed out to the rescue. Back on the sand, they tried vigorously to resuscitate Duncan while Catherine and Sarah looked on, praying. An ambulance screamed up to take him to hospital, while his wife and children were escorted to the police station to await the news. Within ten minutes the call came. Duncan had not recovered consciousness. He was dead.

The accident could have been so easily prevented. There were two red flags on the beach but, according to Maria and George, they were small and ragged. The morning after the accident, they were replaced with a large red flag on a tall pole. Manos Holidays offered their condolences to Mrs Parker but insisted that Duncan and all the other guests had been warned about the currents by the company rep at the welcome meeting. A warning, they said, had also been sent to the family with their tickets and was repeated in their information booklet. The beach was perfectly safe – except when the red flag was flying.

The lessons to be learned here are obvious. Read about your holiday destination, and concentrate in particular on the smaller print. Holiday companies do not want to scare tourists off, and so do not like to play up a resort's dangers. Aside from a kids' pirate holiday, you won't see brochures stamped with the skull and crossbones, even if they really ought to be. So, as is said so often throughout these pages, take responsibility for your own well-being. You are, after all, the only one you can really trust.

The one without Seaman Staines

It's commonly held by those who like a laugh that one of the great works of English literature is Jerome K. Jerome's *Three Men In A Boat*. Though first published back in 1889, this tale of a trip up the Thames in the company of Harris, George and Montmorency the dog retains an extraordinary freshness. The idle gang's foolish mistakes could be committed by any one of us today. Their misadventures could still befall us all. Even their little tragedies are far from being beyond the realms of today's possibilities. Indeed, so many over the last century have enjoyed this hilarious tale of messing about on the river that countless numbers have followed its course for real, and we continue to do so in this new millennium. Don't we all love the notion of a slow trip upstream, gazing out across the feathery reeds and over-hanging willows, watching the ducks lazily bobbing and the insects skating crazily over the water, simply luxuriating in the hazy bounty of summer? It's in our national consciousness. We all, at some point, feel like a bit of a punt.

These were the thoughts of Jane and John Milton when they decided to sample the marvels of Yorkshire's Leeds-Liverpool Canal. They would hire a boat from Pennine Marine and spend a week gently chugging through the wilds and wonders of one of the country's most picturesque regions. And they weren't silly about it, either. Many inexperienced folk have fallen foul of water's manifold eccentricities and Jane and John were not keen to join their number. No, they would take their vacation with two close friends, veterans of several boating holidays. That way they could find their feet and maybe, later on in the week, they might don the captain's hat themselves.

It was a good plan, and all went well. Drifting through the verdant landscape, they enjoyed the lush foliage passing slowly beside them and the wind-blown blossoms resting prettily on the water. They relished the call of the wildfowl and the gentle lapping at the bank. And they were careful to avoid the pitfalls suffered by so many land-lubbers before them. Jane ensured there was a rubber ring for John, a non-swimmer, and he kept it religiously at his side whether he was fore or aft, eating his dinner or lying in bed. Indeed, so loath was he to let the ring leave his sight, Jane thought he might have had some premonition of doom.

If he did, it wasn't a very good one. Three days into the holiday, they reached Bingley Locks. Jane and John stayed onboard, watching carefully as their friends negotiated the five-lock sequence, with the big wooden gates opening and closing, letting the water drain down to the level required for further progress. A little further on came Field Locks, another succession of drops. This time the procedure would be different. Having learned the ropes at Bingley, John and Jane would take the boat through, while their friends manoeuvred the locks themselves.

John felt more than confident in doing this. It seemed simple enough. And it was – he took the boat through the first lock without a hint of a hitch. Then they entered the second lock. At this stage, Jane stepped off onto the canal bank. She said she didn't like the sensation of sinking as the boat dropped to the lower levels. But maybe it was another premonition as the boat suddenly began to tip at the front. The friends at the lock's controls shouted for John to keep the boat forward and, by God, he was trying. Unfortunately, the rudder was caught on the previous lock's gate and refused to break free, tipping the boat at an ever more pronounced angle. Everything inside the boat came crashing down, the sound of splintering crockery filling the air. Black smoke began pouring from the boat. A look of absolute horror spread across John's face and, now nearly lying on the back of the cabin door, he watched the boat keel sideways and instantly sink. 'It went down like the *Titanic*,' said Jane later, 'And I'm not Kate Winslet and John's no Leonardo DiCaprio.'

Thankfully the water was not deep, and John survived unharmed. But in mere seconds £12,000 worth of damage had been done. Though lying in the shallows, the boat was filled with water. All the drawers of clothes were soaked, cameras were destroyed and mobile phones. Jane and John drove home that afternoon with their money drying on the dashboard of their car. While on the M6 they discussed what they could possibly say to the neighbours. They'd told everyone they were going for a week and here they were returning on Monday. It would look suspiciously like they'd buggered everything up. After much to-ing and fro-ing, they decided to tell the truth.

When they popped next door to pick up their keys, their bemused neighbour asked, 'What have you done? Have you sunk it?' Jane replied with what John considered a rather smug affirmative. As it turned out, she'd told everyone they knew that he'd be in the water by Tuesday and was secretly delighted that he'd made it a day early. Naturally, given the sympathy one traditionally receives from one's friends and neighbours at such moments of crisis, John was henceforth known as Horatio, though some referred to him as Captain Pugwash.

Discussing the incident, Pennine Marine were quick to point out that all hirers of their boats are given clear safety instructions and the waterways code. If these had been followed the accident would certainly not have occurred. British Waterways, meanwhile, stated that over 500,000 people every year enjoy a canal holiday without sinking their vessel. To Horatio, of course, this information was of no consolation at all.

The one with not enough water

Though they're springing up everywhere these days, the real home of the water park is the Mediterranean. Maybe it's the heat, or the endless, clear blue sky, or even the righteous hangover you get from too much of the local red wine. But after a few days in a Med resort even the most lethargic among us is ready and willing to fly head-first down a monumental slide into a pool of cool, cool water. Water parks are fun, they're refreshing, they're a magnificent combination of Mankind's ingenuity and Nature's limitless bounty. We should thank God every day for water parks. Like Labradors, Leonard Cohen and haslet sandwiches, they make a marked contribution to the pool of human joy from which we all gratefully sup.

So it seemed to Milly Simm and her husband Charles when they took their annual holiday on Mallorca. They'd wanted to experience a young and lively place and they'd certainly found one in the Balearics. The nights were filled with fine foods and wine, with singing and dancing. The red-hot days were packed with pedal-boats and sightseeing. They gazed from their lofty balcony down onto a teeming world of happiness. It was a great holiday – no doubt about it.

On the final day, though, it was cloudy. The sand and the sea had lost the sparkle lent by the burning sun. So, as you do when your spirits need a lift, they decided to visit the local water park – Aquaworld – a mighty development of huge slides, curving shoots and fountains shaped like giant toadstools. Surely this would bring their most excellent vacation to a breathless peak?

They'd been there just ten minutes when it happened. After just a couple of exhilarating rides, Milly decided to try out the Tarzan Swing. The process was simple enough. At the top you grabbed the handles on either side of a rope stretching down into the pool, jumped off the platform and slid happily down the rope into the water – just like you see on a military assault course, but without the inevitably muddy landing. It wasn't even very high.

So up the steps Milly went, filmed all the way by Charles. She pulled the rope towards her, seized the handles and jumped off the platform. But instead of gliding gracefully downwards, the weight of her leap made her hands slip from the handles and she plummeted feet-first straight down into the water. She felt her feet thud against the bottom of the waist-deep pool. An unbelievable pain shot up her leg. She was convinced that a broken bone was now sticking through the skin of her foot. Feeling numb and sick, all she now wanted was the get to the side of the pool to see what damage had been done.

Naturally, Charles was still filming all of this. 'Smile, Milly,' he was saying, 'I'm filming you, you miserable so-and-so.' But as she struggled closer he realised that the look on her face was not one of mopishness or disinterest. She was clearly in excruciating pain. Putting the camera down, he leapt into the water to help her out.

Once out of the pool, Milly didn't dare examine her injuries. Fearing the sight of that protruding bone, she asked her husband to check it and tell her what he saw. And what he saw was no snapped bone and no blood, just an advanced and angry swelling on her left foot. At the hospital, x-rays revealed that, in fact, both feet had been severely damaged. The right was badly fractured, while the swollen left was shattered. A disconsolate Milly wondered if she would ever walk again.

Two days later, she was back in England and undergoing treatment. Afterwards, the surgeon told her that her left foot was beyond repair. To make this very clear to her, he forwarded a uniquely depressing comparison. 'Get a Crunchie bar,' he said, 'stand on it and look at it. Can you repair that? That's what your foot looks like. There's nothing I can do.'

Years later, Milly was still suffering a lot of pain due to the accident, usually around the ankle and heel, with pain firing up her leg. Feeling aggrieved that the water beneath the Tarzan Swing was not deep enough to cushion her fall, she blamed Aquapark for her sorry situation. The owners (actually the previous owners as the park had changed hands since her fall) pointed out that, not only had they paid all her medical expenses, but the water park also conformed to all relevant regulations. The case had been treated as an accident and that was that.

Thus Milly received no recompense for her agonising injuries, and will surely never visit a water park again. It was a double blow, damaging her capacity for both joy and contentment. So, here's a word to the wise – look before you leap. Not even Johnny Weissmuller would have escaped this one unscathed.

7 Better dead than wed?

For all of us holidays are important. Often they're the only chance we have to set our senses free to explore the new and the exotic. Our minds are given the chance to stop obsessing over the dismal minutiae of the working week and worrying about the petty-minded wallies who plague us on a daily basis. On holiday you're not assaulted by neighbours infuriated by the six or seven petals that have been blown from your rose bushes onto their lawn. You're not pestered hourly by cold callers and thoughtless, selfish creeps itching to sell you double-glazing much like the double-glazing you had put in six months ago, thank you very much. On holiday, your privacy is not invaded by weird couples who want to drink your coffee and guide you to the Kingdom of the Lord.

We all love holidays, and we want them to be special. Some people like to make them extra-special by combining them with other special occasions. A trip to Venice on the wedding anniversary, perhaps, or a birthday jaunt to

Amsterdam. And then there's others who go *all out*, who combine the Big Holiday with the Big Day, who actually get married on holiday. We're not talking here about the Shirley Valentines of this world, those benighted women who fall for exciting Greek fishermen only to end up scraping fish scales off his nets while he's down the taverna with the lads. No, this concerns the 40,000 couples a year who spend millions on luxury weddings overseas. These people step way beyond our dreams of a good holiday. They're looking for *perfection*.

Along with 'irony', 'perfection' is one of the most sorely overused words in the English language. When we say 'perfect', we don't generally mean 'perfect', we mean 'all right', 'just about bearable' or 'if this gets any worse I'm going to punch someone in the face'. But people who cross the planet to get hitched *really* mean it. They dream of a day 'without flaw, blemish or fault'. And, of course, this makes them completely insane. There are so many things that can go wrong at a wedding, and by travelling away from home you relinquish control over almost all of them. The chances of disaster multiply exponentially. You are *seriously* asking for it.

The one without Orson Welles

Just one of these prospective calamities is the wedding video. There was a time when people's memories of the day were held on gaudy Polaroids. Or rather the photos were aides-mémoire. We all knew they were just moments captured on film, we understood that they didn't contain the full beauty, glory and hilarity of the occasion. Before that – because it is the curse of Man that he forgets – we'd hold such moments in our minds. They were, for the most part, bright and sweet and became more so with the passage of time. But videos are different. Recording the day with all its sounds and motion, they show things as they were, not as we think they might have been. Videos take the place of memories, yet unlike memories they do not improve with age. This is why they absolutely *have* to be done well. If they're not then people's memories are spoiled, just as surely as if the videomaker had tossed a grenade into the church.

Mind you, you do get what you pay for. £150 isn't going to get you Martin Scorsese, after all. But Marc and Lara Roberts did spend out for the best. They decided to get wed on Margarita, an island in the Caribbean, just off the coast of Venezuela. And how beautiful it was. The weather was wonderful, the resort a picture, Lara looked magnificent. What memories they would have.

When they returned home they couldn't wait to get the video into their player, to relive the moment as soon as possible. Excitement was high as they sat back on the settee to enjoy their wedding all over again. The video began badly as the camera slowly panned down a dirty white tower and across to a nondescript hotel complex, then sped past the bride and groom as if they were some unimportant blot on the landscape. Everything was horribly out of focus and backed with tedious lounge music that would better have suited a Seventies porn movie. Next it cut to Marc helping Lara as, hampered by her delicate wedding shoes, she struggled up the side of a steep bank, at the top of which everyone was supposed to gather for a video-shoot. Marc's dad stepped in with further assistance, both the men holding Lara's dress up as she battled to keep upright on the slope. On the settee, their hearts sank. Surely this could all have been edited out. Far from being beautiful and romantic, the footage possessed a gritty and depressing social realism worthy of the young Mike Leigh. Who wants to star in *Abigail's Party*? *That*'s not what they paid the money for.

And it got worse. Next, the videomaker had taken Marc and Lara to the local zoo, presumably to add an exotic edge to the proceedings, with the happy couple to be filmed strolling through a jungle paradise. Or so they'd thought. In fact, the man was far more interested in the wildlife than the newly-weds, his camera lingering on the flame-red parrots, a hippo, some more parrots and, as Marc bitterly put it 'other rodents running around that you'd never seen before in your life'. At one point, as they walked arm in loving arm across a pretty wooden bridge over a tropical lake, they noticed that he wasn't even looking at them and seemed most surprised when they caught his attention.

It couldn't get worse. But it did: next came the ceremony itself. The wedding vows – to Marc and Lara the most important part of it all. At last the picture came into focus. Could this be a scrap of comfort to seize hold of in their old age? No chance, for the microphone, with startling ineptitude, had been placed directly beside a pretty, bubbling fountain. It sounded like they were getting married in the shower. And the picture didn't remain adequate for long, either. With a touching romantic flourish, the couple had set their wedding rings on two crimson petals on a linen-covered table. The videomaker noticed this and spent several moments zooming in and out, trying to focus on them. When he finally managed a clear picture of this profound symbol of the couple's love, he gave it three-tenths of a second and moved on. Who was this filmic imposter?

Marc and Lara just couldn't believe it. It was so infuriatingly bad. Next they watched themselves walking past a big bin surrounded by photographers, with members of the general public mooching across the video's lens and waving good-naturedly. Then they were posing with flowers and more parrots as the camera shot straight up their bodies and up into the sky, as if the videomaker had been hit on the forehead with a sledgehammer. But this was no accident, it was all a part of the man's artistic style, for the picture flew upwards once more after catching them on a grassy verge beside some parked cars.

This wasn't just awful, it was *relentlessly* awful. It could have starred Ricky Gervais. Now they're climbing some steps to the reception and Lara catches her heel and nearly falls. Now they're sitting on a small triangle of grass with jeeps driving past, and the camera careers backwards as if the videomaker is on the back of a speeding motorbike. Finally, as if all this were not enough, came the *pièce de resistance*, the cinematic crescendo – the cutting of the cake. Marc and Lara stand together, two hands on one knife, two hearts with one future, and the camera moves down to focus on two flies sitting happily on the icing.

Now, it might be that this video has simply been misunderstood. Perhaps, like *Citizen Kane* before it, it will be held up in years to come as a piece of artistic genius that dwarfed all works before and after it. But even so, it wasn't what Marc and Lara asked or paid for. They were devastated.

First Choice, with whom they'd booked their wedding package, pointed out that their brochure had clearly stated that video quality might differ from UK standards. What it *hadn't* stated was that Marc and Lara would have got a better wedding video from a drunken blind man with epilepsy. The Roberts would receive £160 in compensation. They would probably have valued their memories a lot higher than that.

The one with the reluctant angel

Lance and Jo Wardly were another couple to suffer at the hands of a screamingly inefficient film-maker. They too had booked a First Choice wedding package, this time on Cyprus. As with the Roberts, they held the video to be of paramount importance. 'I thought,' said Jo later, 'I would want to play it over and over again for the rest of our lives.' Beyond this, once they'd returned from that beautiful island back home to Mansfield, she and her new husband were aching to show the footage to friends and relatives who'd been unable to make the trip. So – horrifyingly, as it turned out – they weren't alone when they slid the vid into the player.

Straight away, they knew they were in for trouble. The video opens with a shot of Lance and his father's wife standing in the doorway of the town hall. It is not clear what is happening, and it's all the less clear when some woman who obviously has nothing to do with the wedding bumbles between them and the lens. Quickly we cut to the blushing bride herself. Good thinking, cameraman, let's get straight to the nitty-gritty of this auspicious occasion. And, by God, does she look beautiful in her £1000 dress, like a princess from a far, far better world than this. Unfortunately, the impression is only momentary. When the bright sun of Cyprus hits that dress the viewer is all but blinded by the ferocious glare. Now poor Jo is unrecognisable, though you might take a fair guess that she is an avenging angel of the Apocalypse.

Next the videomaker takes them down to the beach for a touch of sunny romance and local colour. Another smart move, it seems. Why get married in Cyprus, after all, if you're just going to stay in some nondescript registry office? But the videomaker is clearly not simply interested in capturing the moving conjunction of two star-crossed lovers. Where Jo was picturing herself promenading through pretty archways garlanded with wild flowers, the man behind the lens instead shows her struggling to get her dress through a two-foot hole in a low concrete wall. Where she imagined herself embracing her beloved on the white beach with a luxuriant Mediterranean backdrop, he shows her struggling across the sand in her massively inappropriate ballerina's footwear, moving rather like a drunken mallard.

Watching this horror unfold, Jo was already in tears, while Lance was itching to smack the film-maker on the nose. Sadly, they would rapidly be made to feel even worse. Still at the beach, the videomaker makes a surprising decision as to what exactly constitutes local colour. Panning across a beach crowded with sunbathers, he lingers pervily on any topless woman he can spy. 'Don't get me wrong,' said Jo much later, 'I'm not a prude. But not on your wedding video …'

And on it goes. Back at the hotel, Jo and Lance make their grand entrance into the reception, to the sound of cheers and applause. But now, with the light reflecting harshly off the hotel's walls and the cameraman still not remotely concerned with the notion of over-exposure, Jo's dress has changed colour. She now resembles a huge, irradiated canary. Soundtracking this ghastly vision, the traditional wedding music fades wildly in and out, giving the viewer a churning sensation that's as unpleasant as the pictures onscreen. Suddenly the videomaker decides to ignore the happy couple entirely, and they fall out the side of the shot as some unknown photographer helps himself to a glass of wine.

It was terrible, heart-breaking stuff. And there was still one mighty humiliation left in store. As the newly-weds take a stroll outside the reception (Jo of course resembling a jumbo magnesium flare), we hear the incomparable Tina Turner belting out 'I Don't Want To Fight'. Now what was *that* supposed to mean? Was it in some way echoing the high romance of, say, *Gone With The Wind*, with Jo and Lance as the constantly bickering Scarlett O'Hara and Rhett Butler? Or had they intended to use Tina's 'Why Must We Wait Until Tonight' and just blown it?

Lance was furious, Jo mortified. She'd wanted their wedding video to be a glamorous testament to their love. She'd wanted to be proud to show it to friends and relatives. But it hadn't turned out that way at all. 'When people watch our wedding video,' she said later, 'they laugh. They don't mean anything by that, but they laugh.' It's hard to blame them, but it's equally hard not to commiserate with Jo and Lance. Without a wedding video to play over and over for the rest of their lives, they now celebrate their anniversary by donning their wedding clothes and strolling through the garden. 'The dress still looks good,' says Lance, with an echo of Rhett at his most romantic, 'she looks like an angel in it.'

The Wardlys had paid £1523 for their package and demanded compensation. First Choice refused, so they took them to court. Eventually, they were awarded £300, plus costs.

Looking at it from the outside, this may have all turned out for the best. After all, wedding videos are nice, but surely not as nice as stopping to smell the flowers with your beloved, with the both of you garbed in the same clothes you wore when you first promised your undying love. One you watch, the other you live. So come on – press Stop and get on with it.

The one with the disappearing reception hall

Of all the overseas wedding locations, the Caribbean is perhaps the Brits' favourite. Even though most of the world is now open to us, the West Indies retain their reputation as an exotic and high-class destination. If finances allowed, most would choose to get hitched on the white sands there, and to toast their undying love with tropical cocktails in coconut shells.

So it was with Geoff Roberts and Anna Gummer. They'd been planning to get married for some ten years, yet money had always been too tight to permit them that luxury. But when Geoff was made redundant and received a large pay-off, at last the chance was there. He decided to spend a chunk of his windfall on the wedding of a lifetime, something special for his longtime lover. And the best place he could think of? The Caribbean. When he told Anna he'd booked a cruise-and-stay in the Dominican Republic, she felt like she'd won the lottery. She ordered her dress, handmade over a period of seven weeks, and got everything prepared. All was looking good.

And it stayed that way, too. The first week of their holiday was spent cruising round the fabulous islands of the West Indies. It was an absolute treat. And they continued to have a ball when they finally arrived at the Dominican Republic. The scenery was fantastic, the sun scorching. At the hotel, the pools were arranged so you could swim up to the bar. It just didn't get much better than this.

Anna in particular was ecstatic. After all, she'd dreamt of her wedding day for years and here it was, so close she could almost breathe its sweet scent. Over all this time, her vision of that day had grown and refined itself. In her mind she now saw a beautiful sunny afternoon, manicured lawns, a pergola heavy with tropical flowers, Geoff with a big beam on his face – and here it all was, right in front of her.

How quickly it was all snatched away. The day before The Day, the Dominican Republic was hit by a hurricane. Violent winds swept over the island, hard rains lashed down upon the hotel. The balcony quickly flooded, the water entering their room and rising inexorably towards Anna's wonderful dress. Geoff spent ages out on the balcony, scooping up water in a bucket and throwing it over the side of the hotel. Eventually the wind grew too strong and he had to come back inside to safety.

By the next day, the hurricane had moved on to wreak havoc elsewhere. But it had done its work well. As Geoff and Anna ventured out into the hotel grounds, they saw that the place had been 'obliterated'. Where they were to be married the roof was gone and the destruction within was incredible. Anna's long-dreamt-of manicured lawns looked as if they'd been the victims of a 200-foot mole. The tropical flowers had all had their blossoms ripped away by the furious wind. The pretty palm trees had been viciously uprooted and now lay in crazy shapes wherever the hurricane had carelessly discarded them. Anna's luxuriant dreamscape was like a war zone – but without the Americans shooting at her.

The wedding, of course, was cancelled, and the couple were very upset. They still had each other, but this was a bad blow. 'This shouldn't really matter,' said Geoff later, 'but we'd paid a lot of money and it was for nothing … except to come to a foreign place and be terrified.' Worse still, the storm had severely damaged communication links from the island so Geoff and Anna couldn't call home to tell everyone that the wedding had not taken place. Consequently, they arrived back in Blighty to find their house festooned with balloons and banners shouting Congratulations! and Just Married! When Anna saw the presents and cards so thoughtfully laid out on the sofa, she burst into tears.

A year later, they had still not married. Their Caribbean dream could not be re-arranged, and Geoff believes he'll never be able to afford it. They'd spent £3027 on their wedding package, a lot of money. Thomson said they were sorry for the couple's inconvenience but their brochure did say the Caribbean's weather is unstable between July and October. Even so, they compensated to the tune of £475 for the wedding that never happened.

This sad story does raise an interesting possibility for those who seek extreme experiences or would simply love to get married somewhere really unusual. You know, the kind of people who like to exchange vows after jumping out of aircraft, or clinging precariously to the vertiginous slopes of the Eiger, or sitting in Nemesis at Alton Towers. Rather than being inconvenienced by a hurricane, why not deliberately seek one out? That's right, find a hotel that's about to be severely rogered by a massive storm. Book yourselves in, dress up in all your wedding finery and, when the hurricane hits, hide in a secure spot, along with the registrar or priest or voodoo queen or death cult leader or Darth Vader impersonator or whoever it is that's going to officiate at the ceremony. Wait for a few hours while the windy sod does its worst. Then, when all has gone deathly quiet, race outside, get through the vows as fast as you can (matching the speed of a quicksilver-tongued reggae toaster is advisable here), and then get your married arses back inside before the tempest strikes again. Congratulations. You've just got hitched in the eye of a hurricane. How cool is that?

If you're the sort of thrill-seeking renegade to whom this might appeal, then do read on. Later in this book you'll be told how to safely tie the knot in the middle of a rampaging phalanx of soldier ants, in the belly of a Blue whale at 20,000 fathoms, and in Mike Tyson's en-suite bathroom – without asking him first. You know it makes sense.

The one with the brideless reception

Weddings are complicated occasions at the best of times, fraught with danger even down to the tiniest detail. Will the dress be ready? Will the flowers arrive on time? Will lettuce be OK for those guests who won't eat anything that's been alive? Can we sing 'Jerusalem' at the service even though it reminds Uncle Charlie of that terrible night in Hamburg? Can we get away with sitting Great Aunt Gertrude only three tables away from Cousin Wilbert after he kidnapped her spaniel, shaved it, painted it fluorescent yellow and sent it to her by Recorded Delivery? That's right, it's a nightmare of panicked organisation, an extravaganza of terrified anticipation. And that's if you're just doing it down the local town hall.

Some people, though, have confidence beyond that of mortal man. They deliberately complicate their weddings even further, combining them with international travel and the myriad tribulations that can entail. Such a couple were Nigel and Helen. They fancied, like so many others, a ceremony in the Caribbean. No problem, they had the money. But Nigel was a very proud Scot, and really wanted to hold the reception back home in Glasgow. For the benefit of those who wouldn't be able to make it over to Jamaica, the party would have a Caribbean theme, complete with timpani, cocktails and fancy dress.

Everything was prepared, down to the irrelevant minutiae. The couple would marry in Jamaica, spend a two-week honeymoon out there, then fly directly back for the reception. They allowed easily enough time to get their clothes dry-cleaned and make it to the party in time to greet their guests.

How well it started. Their wedding day was a spectacular success, marked by bright sun, champagne and exotic flowers. They were photographed beaming happily beside their closest friends, then embracing in a hammock on a picture-postcard beach. The two weeks that followed were no less idyllic.

For their return, they made it to the airport in plenty of time. They boarded their aircraft and it began taxiing out across the runway. Fortune was smiling on the blissful newly-weds. But then suddenly the plane stopped dead as the pilot hit the brakes. Everyone had to get off and, after a two-hour wait, they were informed that the plane could not be fixed. They would have to wait for an alternative flight.

Nigel and Helen were obviously concerned, but they knew they'd still make it to Glasgow on schedule if they left by the morning. But as the hours crept by, their hopes began to fade. They called the travel agent, pleading to be placed on one of the other planes leaving for the UK. Couldn't be done. They knew there were planes leaving, they knew they had spare seats, they just weren't permitted to board one of them. How livid were they when the mother of one of their fellow passengers approached and said something like, 'You still here? My daughter was on the one that left ten minutes ago.'

When at last they were placed on a flight and up in the sky, they knew they'd miss the beginning of the reception.

So they were at 35,000 feet when their guests arrived, all in their flowered shirts and Rasta wigs, garlands and straw hats. They were miserably peeling the lid from their re-heated flight-food as the invited sat down for their slap-up wedding banquet. They were toasting each other with tiny bottles of whiskey as their mates and family raised their glasses of champagne to absent friends (actually, they raised their glasses to two mannequins they'd constructed out of balloons, one wearing a tux, the other a white dress).

Finally they landed, still in time to make the first dance. It wouldn't be so bad, after all. Or so they thought until British Airways couldn't find their luggage. Again they waited, only to discover that their cases hadn't showed up. No cases, no wedding dress, no smart black suit. By the time they'd hailed a taxi and were screaming off to the reception, Helen didn't really want to go. It was so far away from her happy imaginings.

But they made it anyway, just in time for the last dance. As they burst in and onto the dance floor, clad in their extremely casual travelling clothes, everyone was cheering and clapping. After all, the guests had come from all over the world and had had a *great* time.

All was not lost for Nigel and Helen, though. They may have missed their own wedding reception, but BA did have the decency to admit their service had not been up to the usual standard. They presented the newly-weds with six return tickets to anywhere in the world. They could extend their honeymoon for *months*.

8 When hotels attack!

There are so many problems to anticipate when travelling abroad. Will the weather be fine? Will the water be drinkable? Will there be proper facilities for the kids? Will the beach be close by? All of these things and many more prey upon our minds before departure. But perhaps the most common fear is that the accommodation won't be up to scratch. We've all stayed in some hell-holes in our time and we pray to God that it won't happen again – not on holiday, that would be too unfair, too awful. Yet it happens to people all the time. Every single moment of every single day, someone somewhere is looking round their holiday accommodation, grimly contemplating man's inhumanity to man. There are some real stinkers out there – here are just a few of the worst.

CHAPTER EIGHT

The one with the repeating bathtub

Gran Canaria – its very name sets it ahead of the other Canary Islands, like Tenerife or Gomera. It is the *Gran* Canaria, the Head Honcho, the Duke, the A-Number-One. Situated slightly above the Tropic of Cancer, it lies just off the west coast of Africa, a relatively short journey from the exotic Moroccan cities of Marrakech and Casablanca. Merely the thought of the place heats the blood, sets the pulse racing and sets free the spirit of adventure. How could you not have a great time in a place like that?

Fairly easily, as it turns out. Yet all looked set fair when Col and Myra Potter arrived with their two young kids. The harbour was sweet and shining, and lined with bobbing boats. The pool was bright and beautiful, filled with happy children splashing about on lilos. Their self-catering apartment was neat and white and more than adequate. They were genuinely satisfied that they'd made a good choice this year.

But isn't this always the way? Isn't it just at the moment when we feel most secure and content that the flames of the underworld begin to lick around our complacent toes? This was certainly the case with the poor Potters, for trouble was brewing from Day One.

It began with the smell. Now, smell isn't necessarily a

problem. You wouldn't complain if your flat was infused with the aroma of newly baked bread, or freshly cut jasmine. But this wasn't a nice smell. It conspicuously failed to carry the sweet scent of summer lawns, or even the deep, earthy redolence of woodland moss. This was a stink, a pungent stench, as if someone had boiled rotten eggs and carelessly let the water steam away to nothing. As Col himself put it, it was 'that usual Spanish smell but a little bit more ... rancid'. Every morning that putrid pong assailed them as they used the bathroom. They sprayed and wiped and scoured, they tried bleach, creams and anti-bacterial agents. Nothing, it seemed, could clear the mephitic air. The reek just got stronger and stronger and stronger.

Even then they could bear it. Keeping true to that great British attitude that tells us to Pack up your troubles in your old kit bag, Smile though your heart is breaking and, er, Come into the garden, Maud, they battled through it. The weather was so lovely they didn't spend much time in the apartment anyway and, hey, even the vilest whiff won't disturb you when you're asleep.

If only it had stayed that way, their bulldog spirit might have seen them through. But it didn't. One day Col flushed the toilet and heard a repulsive gurgle emanating from the bathtub. Peeking over the side of the tub, his curiosity quickly turned to horror and disgust as yellowy-brown water began to burble up through the plug-hole.

And infinitely worse than the sickening liquid, remembered Col, 'there were other things floating in it – small things, *curly* things'. And tissue, added Myra.

It was now quite obvious what the stench was and where it was coming from. Col went to their holiday rep but, amazingly, was not taken seriously. These things happen when you're abroad, you know. Don't worry, it's only a one-off. It'll all settle down and you won't be troubled again.

What troopers those Potters were. They took the rep's word for it and soldiered on, despite being a tad scared to go back in the bathroom for fear of the little brown monsters that might lie in wait. And all went well. Until it didn't. One afternoon, the family were all in the bathroom, the kids in the bath playing with their toys and Col and Myra enjoying their offspring's watery delight. Suddenly, like a man-hole cover with Godzilla passing beneath, the plug shot upwards and the raw sewage made a spectacularly revolting return, this time jetting into the bath-water along with the kids. It was an outrageous brown blasphemy against the sacrosanct family tradition of bath-time! Col leapt to jam the plug back into its hole and the children were pulled to safety, but this had gone far enough. After all, there's a definite health risk to having your kids bathe in other people's excrement. Col was taking no more. He went straight to the director of the camp and made his feelings plainly felt. No longer would he and his family tolerate living beside a poop volcano.

This time his complaints were recognised and workers from the Spanish equivalent of Dyno-Rod soon showed up at the apartment. According to Col, they were good workers, pretty efficient. They dug up the garden and released the blockage – problem solved. The Potters need never again fear an eruption of Number Twos.

And the plumbers were as good as their word. The bathtub did indeed remain dormant throughout the rest of the family's holiday. Yet Col and Myra's problems were far from over because, when the plumbers were clearing out the sewers, they didn't just release the blockage. There was something else down there, just as distasteful and yearning for freedom. Col was the first to see. Passing through the bedroom, he thought he spied out of the corner of his eye something moving. No, that's not quite accurate. It was *scuttling*. Col says he's not scared of much but will admit that, when he looked up and saw sitting on the curtain rail the biggest cockroach he'd ever encountered, he very nearly hit the ceiling. He was shaking as he approached the enormous insect, with its glistening armour and flickering chaos of legs and antennae. Catching it in a glass was one of the hardest things he ever had to do.

It was a job he'd have to perform many more times before the holiday ended. The cockroaches were popping up from everywhere, and Col and Myra were much disturbed. Would they creep over the utensils with their sewage-soaked legs? Would they crawl upon the children as they slept? It was all too horrible to contemplate. Col in particular felt he'd let the whole family down, bringing them to this place. He couldn't wait to get home and forget it ever happened.

The Potters paid £1062 for their smelly, bug-ridden vacation. Thomson said they were sorry for the family's inconvenience, but had no record of a complaint. Nevertheless, they compensated to the tune of £660. But was that even remotely enough? As mentioned above, bath-time is one of the few times when a young family can come together with a single shared purpose. The tub is a place of joy, of play and of education. That tub is sacred and the Potters' had been hideously defiled. How could they ever again put their children in the bath without thinking of ... no, let's not think about it again.

The ones with all the hammering

The housing industry is, as you know, worth billions. And there's plenty of wannabe developers out there, desperate to knock up a batch of over-priced dwellings where once the wild flowers grew and the birds sang in the sparkling hedges. Anyone who lives outside the big cities will have recent experience of quaint cottages with beautiful gardens being ripped up and replaced with blocks of £250,000 houses, spaced less than five feet apart. But developers only make money from house sales once. Those who build hotels can make regular cash for decades. The mathematics are simple. The more rooms you have, the more you can let out, the more money you make. So it is that the great Mediterranean holiday centres are often hives of frantic construction activity.

Considering this, we don't find it unusual to see a few giant cranes at work in a resort, to hear the sound of drills in the distance. These things do not bother us – as long as they stay in the distance. But sometimes, when time is of the essence, and a developer is late in getting his hotel ready for the season, that distance can become terrifyingly short.

Take the case of Dave and Caroline Hill. They booked a holiday in Cyprus through Evergreen, a company specialising in vacations for the over-fifties. When booking, Dave made it abundantly clear that they required a quiet room at the rear of the hotel, away from the noise and the traffic. The quiet was essential, they needed to relax. But on arrival, they discovered that their room was not at the rear of the hotel, it was directly above the entrance. This just wasn't on, particularly once the palaver below ensured they had no sleep at all on their first night.

The next morning, Dave demanded that they be given what they'd asked for, a quiet room at the rear of the hotel, over-looking the pool. He could not have known that they were stepping out of a sizzling frying-pan into a raging inferno. The trouble began as soon as the hotel granted their request. The view from their new room was nice – but only if you blocked your ears with Polyfilla and stared straight at the pool, with your palms held beside your eyes to cut out peripheral vision. If you didn't, you became instantly aware that all was not as it should be. Some rooms were not yet complete. More specifically, the room next to Dave and Caroline's was not complete. Worse still, gangs of burly men with power tools were trying to complete it. They'd taken the door off the stairwell for easy access, they'd pulled out the room's window so they could tip wheelbarrows of rubble directly down into the courtyard. Within plain sight of the holiday-makers were piles of smashed plaster and broken planks.

Yet the general unsightliness was nothing compared to the ungodly racket. From 7.30 in the morning till 6.30 in the evening, they were subjected to an ear-splitting cacophony of shuddering drills, cracking hammers, falling debris and roaring engines. It was unbelievable. They were spending their 'quiet, relaxing' holiday in the middle of a building site, and were forced to spend their days in the relative comfort of another hotel.

Eventually, Dave, who'd been extremely wound up by the affair, announced that he'd like to go home. This made Caroline most uneasy, for her husband was a strong man with a forceful personality who never gave up a fight so easily. His claims that he'd take revenge when he got home did not soothe her mind. And how right she was, because Dave fell suddenly ill and, having been admitted to a clinic in Cyprus, died the next day of a heart attack. It had all been too much.

Caroline, naturally, was distraught. Life back in Blackpool would now be infinitely harder but she would fight on, just as Dave would have. Her struggle was not made easier by Evergreen. Refusing to apologise (that would infer some kind of guilt), it took them fifteen months to reach a settlement. Dave and Caroline had paid £1200 for their nightmare, Evergreen agreed to repay Caroline £600. In order to free herself from anger so she could move on into the rest of her life, Caroline decided to forgive them. For that she deserves our wholesale admiration. Evergreen, meanwhile, went into liquidation. A kind of justice was done.

Sadly, the Hills are not the only ones to have suffered from noise pollution. Peter and Tim are musicians, members of a bar-band working on a nightly basis. Along with their wives, Marianne and Sue, they're at it 24/7. So, living a rock and roll lifestyle such as this, when they go on holiday all they demand is total peace and relaxation. And this is what they were expecting to find when, through Club Travel 2000, they booked apartments at the Scorpio complex in Gran Canaria.

To start with, it looked great. Terrific views over a wonderful harbour, a glorious pool with a terrace bar, they thought they were in for a super week. They went straight to their rooms to get a couple of hours' shut-eye before they got down to the business of pleasure.

They did not enjoy the silence for long, After some thirty minutes the horrendous racket began, the vibrations from some huge pneumatic drill shaking the very beds on which they lay. Rushing out onto the balcony they saw three men in floppy hats, busily drilling and hammering away at the concrete base of next door's balcony. One man offered them a big grin and a cheery thumbs-up. They looked around for a hidden camera, as this must surely be some comic set-up, but there was none. They asked one of the workmen how long they were going to be there. One week, he replied. It was, by diabolical coincidence, exactly the length of the families' stay. The workman then had a question for them. 'You just arrived?' Yes, they had. 'You go out tonight?' Yes. 'Disco?' Perhaps. 'Drinking?' Almost certainly. 'OK. Tomorrow morning, nine o'clock, BOOM BOOM BOOM!' You had to appreciate the fellow's sense of humour.

They tried to get themselves moved, but the only alternative on offer was the room directly above their own. The irrepressible Sue burst instantly into the opening of 'The Sound Of Music'. All they could do was plan to keep one step ahead of the builders. They were up and out each day by 8.30. They had fun, they enjoyed the water slides with the children, but most of the time their dog-tiredness took the edge off their amusement. They'd paid £299 each to endure this deafening clamour and, after complaining to Club Travel 2000, they accepted a £300 discount on a future holiday.

Then there was Sarah Hartley and her aunt Tricia Hewson. At a cost of £2820 they booked, through First Choice, a big family holiday in Tunisia. On the coach to the hotel, they saw ahead of them a 150-foot crane looming over a major building site. Quiet whispers began to circulate but no one dared speak their horror's name. This couldn't mean … they wouldn't have … no, it just wasn't possible.

But when they climbed the steps up to their apartments, they discovered that it could, they would and it was. The complex was a huge square with a courtyard in the middle, with their rooms looking inwards. To the right side of them and directly in front, the walls had been torn off completely. All the rooms, rows and rows of them, were empty concrete boxes, decorated only with rubble and twisted steel. Overhead, that mighty crane was swinging an enormous bucket. They had landed in the middle of a major redevelopment.

Of course, they went directly to their rep to complain, and the rep diligently made up a report. But there was no mention of moving to somewhere less, er, *industrial*. They were told they'd just have to make a complaint when they got home. So there they were, marooned on Planet Dust. The din began at 6.30 in the morning and continued all day, rising from a general hubbub to out-and-out pandemonium. There was nothing they could do but try to laugh their way through it.

On their return, they wrote to First Choice. In fact, they wrote four times. Eventually, the company apologised and said it had sent them a letter about the building work, but it had clearly not been received. This wasn't convincing, given Sarah and Tricia had booked the vacation fourteen months in advance. They were offered £900 in compensation.

The letter they hadn't received was very important, legally speaking. By the industry's code of conduct, you have to be notified if your holiday is likely to be disturbed by building work. If you have not been notified you can ask to be moved to another hotel, or even cancel there and then and get your money back. But you must make your complaint immediately. Otherwise you too will pay good money for a vacation similar to spending a week in Motorhead's bass-bins. Ouch.

The one with the disintegrating hotel

Like most of us, Jeff Johnson and photographer Clara Pincer work hard. And when they go on holiday they like to do so in style. It's not that they're after Parker Meridien-style super-luxury, just something really nice, a hotel that's pleasing to the eye with just a few exhilarating facilities. In short, something better than home.

It's not much to ask, and it's relatively easy to find. So when they went down to their usual travel agent they didn't spend long picking out the Elounda Marmin hotel on Crete. The list of its delights was long and impressive. It boasted a private beach, two swimming pools complete with bars, glorious buffet food, options for boating and parachuting, two tennis courts, an open-air theatre and facilities for volleyball, basketball and mini golf. From the photos it looked like a classy joint. Booking through Golden Sun, a company offering 'Holidays to love and remember', they took it.

On arrival they found the resort breath-taking, with the mountains sweeping down to the sea, where lay a beautiful harbour further enlivened by the pretty sails of the boats. Approaching the Elounda Marmin, though, their suspicions were raised by the name sign-posted on the hotel's front. Loose and wobbly, the lettering instantly reminded them of Fawlty Towers. Another bad sign lay in the car park, where a battered old motor crouched on four flat tyres. It had clearly been there some time.

Having checked in, their journey to their room was equally dispiriting. There were stains on the corridor carpets, as if an incontinent moose had recently passed that way. On the ceilings, lights were not properly attached. On the walls electric wires were hanging free. There were deep, crumbling holes in the plaster around the door-frames. Things were looking bad, and they hadn't even got to their room yet.

They opened their door with some trepidation, and their fears were immediately confirmed as accurate prophecies. The ceiling was peeling and far from clean. The wall behind the TV was covered with gross yellowy patches, as if it had once served as the floor in a public urinal. Under the mattresses, the beds were bare concrete, and the sheets were damp and manky. The air conditioning sounded like a road-digger's drill. It would obviously have to be left off at night. And if this wasn't depressing enough, there was the shower. To use it you had to step into a shallow circular basin but, since the curtains only reached down to knee-height, you couldn't help but leave the bathroom floor under two inches of water. It was so ridiculously awful they didn't notice for a while that the light switch had come away from the wall. Oh, well, they thought, we won't be spending much time in the room anyway. Let's go check out those kick-ass facilities.

They began with the crazy golf course, and crazy it indeed turned out to be. Rather than the usual collection of green felt holes scattered prettily among swathes of bright green grass, what they found was several humps of rubber set on raised slabs of badly decayed concrete, all set in a scruffy red-dirt yard stubbled with scrubby plants. The table-tennis room was, if anything, worse. Here the table stood on filthy, broken tiles, the thick dust being moved around by the breeze passing through the smashed windows.

This wasn't a luxury hotel, it was a scene from *Beneath The Planet Of The Apes*. There had to be something nice *somewhere*. Next they tried the roof garden, carefully climbing a set of stairs with several steps missing, passing through a room that looked as if it was used for mortar-gun practice, and finally finding themselves in a wide concrete expanse, bare apart from the carcasses of what appeared to be ancient extractor fans.

Their search for the hotel's one acceptable facility continued. They tried the first pool. Nothing doing – the bar was evidently out of use, with wires hanging loose, floor tiles smashed and a couple of buckets to catch the dripping water. Maybe the second pool ...

They'd found it! The second pool was almost exactly as it appeared in the brochure. Inviting blue water with lovely palm trees and comfortable sun-beds all around. Settling down with sighs of satisfaction (and some relief) they spent the rest of their first day beside this oasis of adequacy.

But, unhappily, their new-found joy was not to last. When on the second day they returned to the pool, they found members of staff hooking dead rats out of the water. What a bummer! They couldn't possibly swim here again, not if there was a chance of coming eyeball to eyeball with vermin from the sewer. Still, there was that private beach to explore. In the brochure, it had looked like the hotel's crowning glory (and, by God, it needed one).

The track down to the beach, lined with twisted wire fencing on the verge of final collapse, did not promise much. And it didn't deliver, either, for the private beach was a blasphemous parody of a Cretan paradise. The decrepit jetty was all rusting iron and broken stone slabs. Beside it, a stray cat sat unhappily beneath ugly, low-set trees that would have been more appropriately placed around the House of Usher. Big holes in the walkways meant that a hard hat would be more suitable than a sun hat. Over in the sunbathing area, the white parasols had been blown from their poles and now hung raggedly from the trees. All the sun-beds were broken, with half their slats snapped or disappeared. The lads quite poetically (and rightly) commented that it looked like a sun-bed graveyard. And, over in the corner, a tall beach shower with no spray attachment dropped a continuous dribble of water onto the grey, cracked ground. The place was shabby beyond comprehension.

Clara and Jeff complained twice and each time were moved to different rooms. At no point did the Elounda Marmin come up to expectations. In fact, it wouldn't have met the expectations of prisoners of war in a Japanese camp in Burma during World War II. On their return, they wrote to Golden Sun detailing the hotel's myriad defects. The company wrote back, explaining that as it was the end of the season things weren't quite in mint condition. Mint condition? Dilapidation like that requires years of conscientious neglect. The lads had paid £898 for two weeks' half-board and wanted their money back. Golden Sun did eventually admit that there had been problems at the hotel, which had now been refurbished. They offered a refund of £440. Clara and Jeff would reject the offer and pursue the matter further.

The one with the regurgitated vegetables

We Brits are notorious moaners. We seldom complain, just moan. And one of the things we moan about continually is the temperature. We're either shivering like slapped jellies or flopping about like junkie sloths. Indeed, extensive research has proven that for the Brits there is only a 1.3 degree gap between too hot and too cold.

Yet the temperature was of no concern to Norman and Helen when they and their kids took off on an Airtours trip to Malta, that gorgeous rocky outcrop nestling below Sicily in the Mediterranean. The island was reported to be sweltering under a heat wave, but the family had no fear. Their hotel, the Qawra Palace, was fully equipped with air-conditioning. Beyond this, it had spectacular views out over Salina Bay, a large pool sitting above the coves of the beach, and it was mere walking distance from the friendly and lively town of Bugibba. Or so the brochure claimed.

What the brochure didn't mention was that most of the rooms did not enjoy that breathtaking bay view. In fact, most of the rooms looked out into an inner courtyard, where the balconies of hundreds of apartments jutted out, each just a few feet from the next, and all of them decorated with drying beach towels. You could see right into most of them – not good when you're accompanied by children of an impressionable age. Privacy levels were set at absolute zero.

Now, you don't have to be clinically diagnosed as paranoid to think people are looking at you when you live in a glass-fronted room surrounded by hundreds of other glass-fronted rooms. It was most uncomfortable, more nerve-wracking than relaxing. Worse, though, was the pong. With all those extractors pointing into an enclosed courtyard already trapping the hot air, the smell was strong, fetid and all-pervading. Norman, showing no sympathy for anyone's finer sensibilities, described it as being like 'warm vegetables which someone's brought up'. His wife concurred, saying it was like cabbage and sprouts, cooked and left to rot. It quickly got so bad that merely stepping onto the balcony made you want to bring up some warm vegetables of your own.

Seeking some respite from the noxious niff, they tried the bar and restaurant. This at least didn't reek of putrefying parsnips, but it did have other drawbacks – no windows just being one. Beyond this, the paint was peeling from the walls and the air conditioning was struggling to cope with the heat wave's extra demands. The perspiration was running from everyone in rivulets. The staff were actually encouraging guests to complain to the management about it. About the heat, that is, not the sweating.

Norman did indeed complain about the defects in the air conditioning, demanding that fans be placed in the bedrooms, in reception and in the dining room. Unfortunately, there weren't any fans. Apart, that is, from the ones in the manager's office and behind the Airtours desk. Everyone else was just going to have to sweat it out. Not only that, but they were going to have to tolerate the workmen who now moved in, painting, scrubbing and hammering directly outside people's doors. If they were hot before, now they were hot and bothered.

Norman and Helen, having spent £2757 on their holiday, officially complained to Airtours about all of this, and in particular the view from their balcony. After all, there was no sign in the brochure of all those drying beach-towels. The company said they were working with the hotel to make improvements, and refunded the couple to the tune of £550.

The one with the new antiques

Eager to avoid the banging techno and rowdy delights of most Mediterranean resorts, and schooled in the soothing wonders of Provence by the much-missed John Thaw, more and more holiday-makers are opting for the French countryside. With pleasant rivers burbling through exquisite woodland glades and a vineyard never far away, what could be better than to rent a cottage or villa, then sit back at a quaint wooden garden table liberally laid out with fine red wine, fresh batons and even fresher camembert?

So thought Lee Holder and his brother-in-law Roger when they picked a farmhouse property from the Chez Nous brochure. It was down in the Dordogne in the south west of the country, just to the east of Bordeaux, and it looked wonderful. It was a seriously enticing cottage, packed with antiques, and blessed with a well-kept garden of climbing plants. A gleaming swimming pool sat just a few yards from the back door. Beyond this, the booking firm boasted, the owners were 'renovation specialists'. They could look forward to a full-blown French experience. *Allez les Holders!*

On arrival they found the Dordogne to be just as advertised. It was a rustic idyll, almost too good to be true. The next morning, though, when Lee's son Harry went exploring, they found that the description of the cottage was *definitely* too good to be true. It began with the downstairs radiator that came away from the wall. Next came the dodgy stairs with banisters that fell to the floor at the slightest touch. Bits of panelling fell away in the kitchen. One outside door frame was coming away, the out-houses were dilapidated. Then there was the toilet door handle that dropped off, leaving you stranded in the kazi till someone heard your increasingly irate demands for liberty.

Perturbed by the results of the search, the family changed tack and set about discovering the promised antiques. Nothing stood out, all the shelves were empty. They thought perhaps the settee might stand up to a once-over from David Dickinson, but sadly it turned out to be a sofa-bed, and a distinctly uncomfortable one at that. Not the sort of thing upon which the Emperor Napoleon might have enjoyed a passionate rendezvous with Josephine.

So, no antiques. But there were tiny bugs. Lee, badly bitten in the night, was forced to spray his entire room. Then another problem arose. The family discovered that no more than three electric appliances could be used at any one time. If the washing machine was on and someone was drying their hair – what with the fridge *needing* to be on – the telly wouldn't work. Odd, very odd. Then they noticed the sockets hanging from the walls in the kitchen and the lights hanging shakily from holes in the ceiling. A tad concerned, they sought out the fuse box and found it to be lurking under a flip-up wooden cover outside. The wiring here was in chaos, with cobwebs and bits of trash everywhere. 'Renovation specialist' clearly meant something different in French.

Because of all this, Lee and the family spent as much time as possible away from their idyllic farmhouse. When on their return they complained to Chez Nous they were told that the company had investigated the matter and found that other families had enjoyed the place. There had been no other complaints. The renovation specialists, meanwhile, denied all accusations of incompetence and botch-jobbing and claimed the family caused some of the damage themselves. Other people returned year after year. There had been no other complaints. So, it was *au revoir* to all that money. *C'est la vie, n'est-ce pas*?

The one with the low-flying aircraft

As we all know, often the thought of a holiday can be better than the holiday itself. The glorious vacation we plan and picture in our minds can't usually be replicated in reality. This book is filled with such disappointments. But some people can't be arsed with all that planning and dreaming. They like to wake up in the morning and say, 'Sod it, I'm sick of all this rain. Let's go somewhere were there isn't any'. Or maybe the chance of a break springs upon you without warning. Maybe five of your numbers came up last Saturday night. Perhaps your recently deceased great-uncle Bobby turned out to be less of a swine than you thought. You might be one of those people who do everything at the last minute.

Last minute was the name of the game for young couple Pauline and Robert when they booked two weeks in Tenerife through Cosmos. What they required was days of sunny peacefulness and nights of wine and boogie, and Cosmos seemed to have hit the nail on the head when they placed them in the Sand Club apartments. They had to be beside the beach. Well, hadn't they?

Apparently not. When they arrived at their accommodation they found that the Sand Club had no sand. And no club, either. What it did have, as they discovered when they tried to sleep on their first night, was a loud and easily identifiable noise. It would begin as a quiet whistle that would grow stronger and stronger until it became a bed-shaking roar coupled with an excruciating high-pitched whine. You've guessed it, it was aeroplanes coming in to land. Every fifteen minutes. All night.

The next day they rose, still chipper despite the lack of sleep. They were a positive pair who liked a laugh and they were keen to explore the complex. The first thing they noticed, now seeing their situation in daylight, was that the Sand Club was separated from the airport runway by just a wire fence. When a plane came into land (as they did. Every fifteen minutes. All day) they could see the wheels coming down and read the logo on the side of the aircraft. So much for those days of sunny peacefulness. Little did they know that plane-spotting was the most exciting activity the complex had to offer.

Next up they tried the beach. This had to be seen to be believed. Rather than the picturesque inlet of golden sand and blue lapping waves they'd expected, they found a horrible confusion of grey rubble. From a skeletal line of poles that had at some point been a fence, they scrambled down over the vile lunar landscape to the bleak water. With typical humour and never-say-die spirit, they christened the place Breeze Block Beach, as broken breeze blocks were its major component.

The beach was a grim and forbidding place, yet in a way it was a perfect companion to the complex itself, which Pauline and Robert soon discovered to be a ghost town. It had a real Omega Man vibe – but without the interesting zombies. In a huge courtyard filled with empty tables and chairs, all set up for a party that never came, the young lovers sat eating ice cream and waiting for the tumbleweed to roll past.

But, as we are all aware, night time is the right time, and that's when the Sand Club really let loose. Or so they claimed. What actually happened was this. As a few tablefuls of tourists tried valiantly to make the best of things, two women in ill-fitting French maid costumes clumsily attempted the can-can. Pauline and Robert found themselves laughing at the performance, but out of pity and embarrassment rather than any sense of enjoyment. It got worse when the women stripped down to pink pointy bras and tiny plastic skirts to mime to Barbie Girl. This had become stag-night fare and Pauline was not impressed.

The next day came a respite of sorts. Exploring a nearby complex (as they'd had more than enough of their own), the couple discovered a beautiful pool and spent the day lounging, swimming and generally enjoying themselves in the sun. 'But still,' you can hear Robert laugh on the video footage they took there, 'we have the *problem*!' And overhead, destroying all thoughts of calm and relaxation, screams another 737.

After a week of this brain-rattling rumpus, they could take no more and went home. When they complained to Cosmos, they were told that, though the company was aware that the resort was over-flown by aircraft, this had never been 'a significant source of complaint'. They probably couldn't hear the complaints for all the noise. In a fit of generosity they offered Pauline and Robert 10% off a future holiday. Camping in Piccadilly Circus, perhaps. Or bivouacking on Platform 12 at Clapham Junction.

This story is definitely worth considering. There is always a chance that, if you book late, you'll get a bargain.

But there's a better chance that all decent accommodation will be booked up and you'll be banished to some wretched, lonely outpost upon which the bright light of fun has never fallen. Make it plain to the travel agent when you book – 'On this holiday I want to see myself as Patrick Swayze in *Point Break*, *not* Gary Cooper in *Beau Geste*. OK?' They'll surely listen. Won't they?

The one with all the rioting

There are several popular conspiracy theories pointing to the existence of secret sects that plot to dominate the world. The Jews have suffered from this for centuries. Nowadays people stab suspicious fingers at the Masons and the Scientologists. Some even believe in a power elite, including among their number George Dubya Bush and his little friend Tony Blair, who occasionally meet in exclusive, secluded American hotels to discuss the details of their devious masterplan.

Of more concern to readers of this book, though, is the theory concerning a new axis of evil that has surreptitiously sprung up within the holiday industry. It's a good theory, too. Indeed, with all the evidence on show, there can surely be no doubt in anyone's mind that there is some form of clandestine competition going on between many hotels across the planet. The idea, so the theory goes, is to see who can best degrade, frustrate and humiliate British tourists while still making pots of cash. Please think before you scoff. In the normal scope of things people don't leave their fellow men to wallow in such pits of filth and deprivation, not on such a large scale. Not unless their name is Margaret Thatcher, anyway.

No, this must be some crazy and cruel global game. Without even knowing it, British tourists are acting as competitors in an international Endurance programme, being pushed and pushed until they leave, break or, in typical British fashion, simply pay up without a word of complaint. Then, at some pre-ordained time of the year, all the participating hoteliers get together and compare video footage of the holidaymakers they've tested, taunted and tortured. Prizes might include Most Ramshackle Plumbing System, Most Rude And Unhelpful Receptionist and Most Convincing Semen Stain On A Mattress. We're not sure exactly what the prizes are presented for yet, but hopefully a full exposé of this shameful award ceremony will be printed in later editions of this book.

One participant must surely be the Hotel Mallorca, naturally enough on Mallorca. It was so awful it even made the papers back in the UK. When Lucy and Liam, Laura and Sarah, and Vince and Alexa all made last-minute phone bookings with Sun Private, they were promised an all-inclusive package in a three-star hotel just 300 metres from the beach. This meant free meals, free drinks, free snacks, free kids club, and free entertainment, with a large pool, tennis courts and a mini-golf course – all for around £285 per person, for a week. You couldn't argue with a price like that. Why, these days that's the price of a train fare from London to, er, somewhere else in London.

When the bus pulled up and let everyone off at the Hotel Mallorca, though, it quickly became obvious how the price could be so low. The two-star sign outside was the first give-away. Then there was the big crack in the glass of the reception door and the lino peeling up off the floor. The place looked grim, perfunctory at best, like a hostel rather than a hotel.

Up in the rooms this impression was confirmed. Rooms for four had four single pick-you-up beds lined up next to each other, with no room to climb in from the sides. Covers were pulled back to find the mattresses soiled, stained and torn. One guest was caught on video saying 'Surely this can't be right. Good God Almighty'. Some burst into tears. In the bathrooms, sinks were cracked and dirty, wall tiles were falling off, wires hung down from the ceilings. There were ants scuttling about the place, toilet seats hanging off. Flushes didn't work, their chains fell off, the fittings were filthy.

Several husbands went straight back down to reception to complain, each listing a catalogue of problems that ended with 'My wife's crying in the room'. Each was told they'd have to wait until the next day to see the rep responsible. Other guests told them they'd be lucky – they hadn't seen him in days. And so they were all condemned to spend the night at the increasingly infamous Hotel Mallorca.

The next day, in the bright Mallorcan sunshine, they had a chance to see the place in its full glory. There were tiles missing from the floors, big holes in the plaster on the walls. Outside there was rubbish everywhere – empty bottles, plastic bags, polystyrene coffee cups all over the place. At the pool the metal frame of the ladder down into the water was not attached to the side. The water itself was cloudy and full of black bits. On top was an odd white scum, dirt was ingrained on the cracked tiles. You couldn't see the bottom.

No one would let their kids in that pool. Standing next to it was bad enough. There with her children, Lucy noticed with disbelief a used condom on the ground. Instead of swimming they tried the kids' play area. But this turned out to be just a rusty metal see-saw and climbing frame set in a small, rough yard covered with a thin layer of sand full of cigarette butts.

And so to lunch. Surely this would be a more joyous experience. The food was free, after all. One look told you why, as everyone had to hunker down to a plate of pink beefburgers and a splodge of half-cooked chips. 'Vile, vile, absolutely vile', was Lucy's tellingly accurate description.

The whole thing was horrible. The next morning they returned to reception to get a hold of the mysterious disappearing rep. The scene this time was very different, for in the night another coach-load had been dropped at the Hotel Mallorca. Some were overbooked, others were refusing to stay in the rooms allocated. The veranda was full of people who'd slept out all night, crashed on plastic chairs and sun-beds. Confused toddlers stumbled weeping through the chaos. 'We would have hired a helicopter, anything, just to get out of there,' said Lucy later, and she, Liam and the kids did soon leave.

The others, though, were stranded, and the hotel was becoming a pressure-cooker of frustration and resentment. Now the rep was here – Juan, a little bald speccy guy without much English. Of course, he was immediately besieged by irate guests who all wanted satisfaction, pronto. It started to get nasty. Juan, stating categorically and finally that he couldn't find any more rooms, suddenly got up and tried to run into his office, but Laura was blocking one door, and Sarah locked another. 'He wasn't getting out, no matter what,' explained Sarah later. Vince was about to grab him when Juan shouted out 'Call the police! Call the police!' It was looking bad for the little rep. One bloke had him by the throat, another was thrusting the phone into his face, demanding that he call someone and *get this sorted out*. Everyone was shouting 'You got them rooms, get *us* one!' Someone was going to get hurt, with Juan the bookmakers' runaway favourite.

Finally the police did show up, probably preventing the first public lynching Mallorca would have seen in many a year. When they left Juan walked out with them. None of the guests ever saw him again. Back home, the newspapers got hold of the story and ran with it. 'Hotel revolt Brits take rep hostage' screamed *The Sun*. The Hotel Mallorca was notorious nationwide.

Nevertheless, one month later another group of Brits turned up to find that little had changed. Once more there was madness in reception. People were furious to discover that there were three beds for four people, there was no bedding, slats in the beds' bases were snapped off. Toilets flushed water all over the bathroom floor. In one room the door handles were broken so the guests had to reach their balcony via the window. The pool was a little cleaner, but still one woman lost her goggles on Day One and didn't find them till Day Eleven. The food was just as unappetising, one woman shooting footage of a dry roll filled with unrecognisable pink meat smeared with white stuff. It could have been ham and cheese. You wouldn't have wanted to try it to find out. Back in reception, everyone was once more looking for Juan. Don't bother, fumed one irate lady, 'All we've had from Juan is "Me not understand, me not understand".'

Juan actually had a very clear understanding of the situation. Interviewed by the *Holidays From Hell* crew, he explained that it was the guests themselves who were leaving the litter, breaking the fittings and making all the mess. It certainly wasn't him, he said.

So *this* was the problem all along. *Damn* those guests. And aside from all the mess, *when* would they learn to cook the food and clean the pool properly? *When* would they ensure they each had a bed and a room to put it in? *When* would they fill in the holes in the walls and fumigate the mattresses? These people were clearly *animals*. They'd come on holiday totally unprepared to muck in and help.

'It's not easy, this hotel,' continued Juan, 'it never work with English people, and I never thought English people were so difficult. For the money you pay you having, more or less, value for money.'

As the guests themselves put it, when you pay for a cheap package you're not expecting the world. But you do expect the place to be clean, and to be able to eat the food and drink the drink. And that does seem fair enough. The guests mentioned above all booked through travel agents Sun Private Limited (now Lane Travel Limited), with the holiday being provided by Real Travel Limited through their agents Access Travel. None of these companies would comment on the difficulties at the Hotel Mallorca. Laura and Sarah would have their money refunded from their credit card insurance. The others pursued claims for compensation.

According to Frank Barrett of the *Mail on Sunday*, you

should be very careful when booking holidays over the phone. To be safe (or safer) you need a written contract with the tour operator – like a brochure. If your vacation turns out bad you can then say the operator promised such-and-such in the brochure and it wasn't like that. If you claim that someone promised you something over the phone, the operators can say '*Who* promised you?' and you'll have no come-back. And, as Mr Barrett stresses, with tour operators you do need a come-back.

So that was the nightmare at the Hotel Mallorca. It seems certain that a year later, at the hoteliers' convention discussed above, the place must have swept the board, like Ben-Hur at the Oscars. And the winner for Most Offensive Poolside Refuse goes to … Juan and the Hotel Mallorca for The Used Condom!! Yeah, definitely a shoo-in.

The one with everyone's poo

Back in the Seventies, one of the world's most popular authors was James Clavell. Most people would have on their bookshelf at least one of his epic adventures – *Shogun* maybe, or *Tai-Pan*. But the one that really caught the imagination of this writer was *King Rat*, the tale of a sneaky procurer in a war-time prison camp. The story was interesting, the psychologies of the characters fascinating, but what got you most, what printed itself indelibly on the memory, was one wholly horrifying description of how the inmates would rid themselves of traitors. They'd throw them head-first down one of the latrines.

Now this is revolting in itself, but Clavell adds further details that have you shaking your head in disbelief. These latrines were, of course, holes in the ground. They were deep and they were narrow. So, if you were unfortunate enough to be thrown in head-first there was no way of flipping over onto your feet and maybe climbing to safety. No, you were trapped, vertical but head-down. All you could do was hold yourself above the pool of excrement until your arms tired and the weight of your body above forced your face under. It's disgusting, isn't it? You couldn't conceive of a more horrible way to die. Except maybe the one with the rat and the hot metal bowl – but that's another story.

Anyway, aside from making absolutely clear that even the most hellish Holiday from Hell is better than life in a prison camp, this story and its effect on the reader affirm our rabid dislike for excreta of all varieties. We Brits take pride in our toilet humour. We jest constantly about our daily functions and post-curry trots, but when it comes to getting down and dirty we really don't like it. When *real* dung enters our lives – dog dung, cat dung, horse dung or, God forbid, human dung – we don't like to deal with it at all. We like to keep it at arm's length. Someone else's arm, preferably.

This is why the experience of Mandy Bolton, her husband and their two sons is so shocking. Aside from the holidays where people actually die, it's by far the most disturbing vacation in this collection. It went like this. The family decided on a major trip to Malta with family and friends, seventeen people in all. It was to be a special trip, a real event. Mandy and her hubbie went out shopping for new clothes specially, the bill coming to around £1000 for the four of them. They had two canvas bags full, stretched to their limit.

They'd booked, through Ryan Tours, into the Cycas apartments in Qawra, a quiet area on St Paul's Bay. It was wonderful, just a minute's stroll from the rocky beach. There was a pool, a bar, a poolside bar, a games room, all the extras they required for a really storming holiday on the lovely island. And, as the brochure categorically stated, there was a full bathroom. Perhaps the Boltons should have asked themselves how full it was going to get.

The first day went swimmingly. They had a superb time at the beach, bathing and jet skiing. It was when they got back to the apartment that things started to unravel. The first sign came when Mandy was taking a shower. Over the splashing of the water she thought she heard a strange bubbling sound, an odd sound she couldn't quite place. Then came a smell, a really strong smell that had her thinking one of the others had entered the bathroom and was, as she delicately put it, 'performing'. She looked out of the shower to see who could be so thoughtless (there were two bathrooms in the apartment), only to notice that the water level in the toilet was rising and the water itself was slowly filling with deep brown faeces. Horrific stuff. They called down to report the incident immediately, a plumber was ordered and dutifully arrived to correct the fault.

The Boltons believed this to be the end of the matter. They'd got to the bottom of it (ho ho ho) and that was to be that. Off they went for a delightful meal and a jolly game of table tennis. A fine evening was had by all. The next morning, though, they awoke to find another bad, bad smell in their nostrils. To their horror, they discovered that the toilet bowl was once again full of noisome excretions. But this time the movements had moved further. Down onto the floor they had crept in the night, then through the bathroom and under the door, before silently slipping into the living area.

This was absolutely unacceptable – these stools were not cool, dude. Once more the Boltons complained, and once more help was quick to arrive. This time it came in the shape of an old lady who instantly got busy with her mop. Unusually, she seemed quite happy to perform her duties in bare feet (bare feet! Can you imagine the horrible squidging between your toes? *Aaaagh*!). The family kept saying to her 'Raw sewage, it's raw sewage', but her only reply as a Manuel-like '*Qué?*'

Naturally, the family demanded to be moved to another apartment. To be evacuated, as it were. Unfortunately, the Cycas, like their unruly toilet, was full to the brim. They'd have to put their trust in Maltese science and, in a manner of speaking, bite the bullet. So, putting their troubles behind them, off they went for a glorious day out on Malta. They took a leisurely boat-trip along the coast, gasping at the pretty coves where the dark rocks dropped steeply into the briny blue. They hired a minibus and driver and checked out some of the gorgeous churches for which the island is rightly renowned. They had a ball.

When they returned, though, they were to face what the Boltons later described as The Big One. The earlier ordure had simply been an hors d'oeuvre. Now came the main course. In their absence, their toilet had misbehaved yet again, and this time it had really done the business. The whole apartment had been flooded with sewage – both bathrooms, the living room, the bedrooms, even the kitchen. Where the bed clothes were trailing on the floor, the evil liquid had soaked its way inexorably upwards. Most of their clothes were still in their canvas bags, sitting on the flooded floor.

As the eruption of excrement had already come to the attention of the powers-that-were (well, you could probably smell it in Sicily), a man was in the apartment mopping up the mess. But somehow the small piles of poop he'd swept together made the disaster all the more heart-breaking. Mandy broke down in tears. Really, her husband had more cause to weep, as it would be he who'd had to go through the bags, feeling and sniffing each item to see if it was steeped in ca-ca. Sadly for him, most of them were.

Now they discovered the gut-wrenching truth. Their toilet was the last stop in the apartment complex's sewage system. This meant that the horrible mess on their floor, in their beds and all over their clothes had passed through the bowels of everyone else on the site. Their rooms had become a giant septic tank. It was unthinkably foul. Their complaints now carried the weight of fury, and they were immediately handed the keys to another apartment.

On their departure, the Boltons left their soiled clothes in Malta. They were thoroughly cleaned and sent over to the family in Blighty, but who'd want to wear clothes that had been dunked in do-do? You'd never feel confident, would you? No matter how well-scrubbed the clothes you'd always suspect that you smelt like you'd been kipping in the gutter of a public urinal. No, the clothes had to go. £1000, in the bin.

When the Boltons had hoped for the vacation of vacations, this was certainly not what they had in mind. Particularly not as the group had coughed up over £6500. Ryan Tours said that they had moved the family as quickly as was possible, and apologised profusely for their discomfort. They were sorry that their clothes insurance was not satisfactory and offered them free accommodation on a future holiday.

The Boltons, meanwhile, became known to their friends as the Poo Family. Their terrible memories of Malta, it seemed, could never be flushed away.

The one with the daddy of them all

During the course of this book, we have come across many a hotel that could easily qualify for the description 'hell-hole'. But there is one hotel, unmatchable in its beastliness and its flagrant disregard for human decency, that conclusively takes the biscuit. This is the infamous Clube Praia De Rocha in the ordinarily rather nice country of Portugal. Brenda Wall of Holiday TravelWatch says that she has received more quality complaints about the Praia De Rocha than any other hotel – they go into the hundreds. And a lot of them concern the incomparably dodgy all-inclusive package.

Hayley and Paula, along with Paula's two little girls, were actually expecting something special. The brochure showed the Praia De Rocha to be a modern complex with a beautiful pool. You could eat breakfast, lunch and dinner at the American-style buffet restaurant, enjoy a nightly poolside barbecue, and avail yourself of unlimited snacks in between. Sounded great – they paid up their £1800 and went for it.

They knew they'd made a mistake as soon as they arrived. Rushed through the lobby to the lifts, they were pointed in the general direction of their room and left to find their own way. It wasn't going to be easy. The brochure had not clearly reflected the size of the hotel. Indeed, comprising 1241 apartments spread over endless blocks, all joined by concrete walkways, it would have required a four or five-page pull-out to do so. The Praia De Rocha has been described as 'Tower Hamlets by the sea' for good reason. It was a vast homogenous warren of stairwells and walkways, all leading out to the different levels of the massive internal courtyards. Hayley and Paula tried hard to follow the signs but still found themselves lost amidst the dark and forbidding towers, with their rows of small, square windows.

At last, they made it to the room. It wasn't good, it wasn't good at all. But despite the dirt and the shoddy furniture and fittings, it was nothing compared to the hotel's other problems. For a start there was the noise. With so many thousands of guests, it was like living in Waterloo Station. Every crash, shout and yelp was amplified ten-fold, with the internal courtyards acting as huge echo chambers. Then there was that American-style buffet restaurant. You'd have to queue up four flights of stairs before you even reached a dining-room that would cause a farm animal to blanch. All the tables were stacked high with used plates and plastic glasses. There were chips and ketchup strewn across the floor. You couldn't get a clean knife and fork for love nor money. Not that you'd want to, for the food was vile – limp, pink sausages and undercooked eggs being the best of it. The guests were evidently being treated as pigs at troughs, and consequently many were behaving in just such a manner.

Even then it was better than the poolside barbecue. Video footage taken the year before Paula and Hayley's holiday shows the chef hooking hunks of chicken out of a big bucket filled with grease and blood (God knows how long it's been sitting outdoors), and chopping it roughly in three. He then tosses it into another bucket, from which it's taken and placed on a huge grill. Taking her portion of chicken and lamb, Paula noticed that it was blood-raw inside. It was a disaster waiting to happen. And, lo and behold, after four days of eating at the hotel, they were all ill with stomach cramps, sweats and diarrhoea.

On their own, Paula and Hayley might have been able to cope. With the kids it was infinitely more difficult. To begin with it was impossible to keep them properly clean. They were pooping themselves all over the place and their apartment had no hot water. They complained to the rep and were told this was probably because everyone in the block was having a bath at the same time. Hmm. For a while they believed this but, as the family grew progressively sicker and the mess greater, with Paula forced to wash her kids down with buckets of cold water, eventually they went to complain again. They *had* to have hot water.

Fortunately, they bumped into a maintenance man who informed them that they could have hot water any time they wanted. All they had to do was flick the switch in their room. Cue fury from Paula. She could not believe that the rep had known so much about all the trips you could take (and for which you'd pay extra) but had not known about this all-important switch.

After two weeks, they were desperate to leave a place where everything was cracked, dirty and wholly uncared for. They were not alone in this feeling. As they left, skipping past the packed bin-liners spilling trash onto the broken-tiled courtyard, many of the guests were literally singing for joy. On their return home, Paula and Hayley added to the list of complaints mentioned above by Brenda Wall. They'd received £180 compensation.

It's amazing that word of the Praia De Rocha did not spread like wildfire across the UK. After all, when someone famous dies or suffers a major humiliation, the inevitable jokes take around twelve hours to reach from coast to coast. You'd think that people would have been keen to pass on the whole sorry story of this horrible hotel.

Yet when Rosie, Matthew and their family showed up for their first family holiday abroad in a decade, they were under a monstrous misapprehension. Rosie, who'd discovered the place, actually believed the Praia De Rocha would be comparable to resorts in Jamaica or the Bahamas. Very quickly her sense of pride and pleasure at finding this hot-spot would turn to guilt and horror. What had she brought her family into?

Aside from the state of their room, breakfast on Day One got them thinking. Matthew opted for the cooked breakfast and received a plate of soggy, undercooked bacon swimming in a soup of disintegrated beans, all topped with a peeled hard-boiled egg. Are you listening, Gordon Ramsay? Biting into the egg, Matthew leapt suddenly to his feet and took off like Linford Christie for the toilet, the only place he could politely spit out his rotten mouthful. It was bad, very bad. But, as one of Matthew's sons suggested, one shouldn't jump to conclusions. Maybe lunch would be better.

Consisting of a gloopy spoonful of repulsive Shepherd's Pie and near-raw chips coated in stinking fat (clearly they liked their spuds), lunch was worse. Rosie and Matthew could not watch their children eating this filth and never returned to the American-style buffet restaurant again. Eating out would cost them an extra £800, pretty much all the money they'd brought with them. It would also cost them much embarrassment. When any restaurant proprietor discovered where they were staying he'd have the whole joint laughing at their foolishness.

Incredibly, Rosie and Matthew had paid £2561 to

suffer the deprivations of the Praia De Rocha. They accepted compensation of £1100, though they may have found that figure derisory if they'd ever made it to the poolside barbecue. Their experience would see Airtours terminating their all-inclusive package deal with the hotel.

Yet still they kept coming. Booking through Sunworld, Angela Jones turned up with her family and was immediately suspicious of the bars at the windows, the barbed wire outside and the broken glass deliberately placed sharp-edge-upwards below their balcony. There was a definite and most unholidaylike prison camp feel to the place. When she found human hair in the sink and what looked like dried blood on the bathroom floor, and she discovered that the promised ocean vista was in fact a view of a dirty brick wall topped with scrubby bushes and yet more wire, she went straight to complain. Finding the reps wasn't easy, but they persisted and demanded to be moved. This was absolutely *not* what was promised in the brochure.

And, incredibly, they *were* moved (it was their right, but under the circumstances it was still amazing). Waiting for information on their new destination, they found themselves sitting with some other couples, then on their last day at the Praia De Rocha. The others were astonished that they'd managed to escape. Wherever they want to send you, they advised, don't ask questions, just go. Anywhere is better than here. *Anywhere*. And so off they went, winding up in a rather fetching self-catering apartment. Of course, they wouldn't have their food cooked for them, but then the food wasn't cooked at the Praia De Rocha either, so no loss there. For their inconvenience, Sunworld repaid £600 of the original £1606 cost. More importantly, their never-say-die attitude had saved them from one of the world's most heinous Holidays from Hell.